An introduction to

The Ocelot and Margay and Other Rare Wild Cats

This publication is Copyright 2015 by EKL Publishing. All products, publications, software and services mentioned and recommended in this publication are protected by trademarks. In such instance, all trademarks & copyright belong to the respective owners.

The moral rights of the author has been asserted

British Library Cataloguing in Publication Data

A catalogue record for this book is available from the British Library

ISBN 978-1-909820-77-7

Disclaimer and Legal Notice

While every attempt has been made to verify the information shared in this publication, neither shall the author nor publisher assume any responsibility for errors, omissions, nor contrary interpretation of the subject matter herein. Any perceived slight to any specific person(s) or organisation(s) are purely unintentional. You need to do your own due diligence to determine if the content of this product is correct for you.

This book is presented solely for educational and entertainment purposes. The author and publisher are not offering it as legal, accounting, or other professional services advice. While best efforts have been used in preparing this book, the author and publisher make no representations or warranties of any kind and assume no liabilities of any kind with respect to the accuracy or completeness of the contents and specifically disclaim any implied warranties of merchantability or fitness of use for a particular purpose. Neither shall the author nor the publisher be held liable or responsible to any person or entity with respect to any loss or incidental or consequential damages caused, or alleged to have been caused, directly or indirectly, by the information or programs contained herein.

The author shall not be liable for any loss incurred as a consequence of the use and application, direct or indirectly, of any information presented in this work. This publication is designed to provide information in regard to the subject matter covered. It is the reader's responsibility to find advice before putting anything written in the book into practice.

References are provided for informational purposes only and do not constitute endorsement of any websites or other sources. Readers should be aware that the websites listed in this book may change. We have no control over the nature, content, and availability of the websites listed in this book. The inclusion of any website links does not necessarily imply a recommendation or endorse the views expressed within them. EKL Publishing takes no responsibility for, and will not be liable for, the website being temporally unavailable or being removed from the internet. The information in this book is not intended to serve as legal advice

An introduction to

The Ocelot and Margay and Other Rare Wild Cats

Colette Anderson

Foreword

When I decided to write about small wild cat species, my original intent was to examine the Ocelot (*Leopardus pardalis*) and Margay (*Leopardus wiedii*). It was a tidy topic confined to a manageable geographic area. So much for planning!

Those two cats are still an important part of this narrative because the species are closely related and easily mistaken for one another. At the same time, however, they present fascinating contrasts in their response to their environment. The Ocelot is a terrestrial animal, while the Margay is an amazing arboreal athlete.

My research made me aware of another cat in the same "neighborhood," however, the Oncilla (*Leopardus tigrinus*). A long-time lover of domestic cats, and a supporter of big cat conservation, I thought I knew my felines. It stunned me to learn of the Oncilla's existence.

I'm supposed to be a "cat person." How did I not know about this elegant little creature? Then I began to understand the elusive nature of the tiny Oncilla, a cat that was not even photographed until 2005, and then only with a motion-activated trail camera.

As is so often the case, one discovery led to another: the Andean Cat, Geoffroy's Cat, the Jaguarundi, Kodkod, and Pampas Cat. I'd never heard of a single one of them.

All told, there are seven species of wild spotted cats living from the southern tip of Texas down through South and Central America. They have a couple of North American cousins, the Bobcat (*Lynx rufus*) and the Canadian Lynx (*Lynx Canadensis*), and, it would seem, a whole host of near relatives the world over.

In no time I was looking at pictures of 32 small cat species scattered around the globe. Some are well known, and many are rare and difficult to study. All, however, are anti-social, regardless of their small size, highly reclusive, and for the most part impervious to domestication – a fact that makes their vulnerability to the pet trade all the more tragic.

Intimately tied to the landscapes they inhabit, their survival is threatened by poaching, habitat destruction, and prey depredation.

The Iberian Lynx, for instance, is critically endangered because disease has largely killed off the rabbits on which they depend. The lynx is so resistant to changes in his diet, that the species is now threatened with extinction.

The big cats command the big conservation bucks. I'm not complaining about that. I don't want to see the mighty tiger disappear from the earth, but neither should the tiny Kodkod or the little Pampas Cat be allowed to go extinct.

I hope by the end of this book you will be moved to support many of the fine organizations working to protect and preserve small feline species around the world. There are far more of them than I realized when I began work on this text, a book that has changed direction three times before arriving in this final form.

Each of these felid species is worthy of our admiration and our protection, but we can extend neither until we are aware of their existence. That is my major goal with this book. In the end, I think your eyes will be opened to a whole new world of small wild cats as mine have been.

Colette Anderson

Table of Contents

CHAPTER 1 – OCELOT AND MARGAY: KINDRED CATS....................1

The Ocelot: A Terrestrial Cat...2
The Ocelot's Habitat 2
Physical Characteristics.. 3
Movement 5
Diet... 6
Cycle of Activity.. 7
Social Behavior.. 9
Communication... 10
Mating and Reproduction 10
Relationship with Other Felids.. 12
Predators.. 12
Ocelots in Captivity 13

The Margay: An Arboreal Cat...15
The Margay's Habitat 16
Diet.. 17
Cycle of Activity.. 18
Physical Characteristics.. 18
Movement 20
Social Behavior.. 22
Communication... 22
Mating and Reproduction 23
Relationship with Other Felids.. 24
Predators.. 24
Margays in Captivity... 24

CHAPTER 2 – SMALL SOUTH AMERICAN CATS...........................27

Andean Cat..27

Geoffroy's Cat...30

Jaguarundi..34

Kodkod 38

Pampas Cat..41

Oncilla 44

CHAPTER 3 – NORTH AMERICAN CATS.................... 50

Puma 50

Bobcat 58

Canadian Lynx 62

CHAPTER 4 – ASIAN CATS................................. 67

Asian Golden Cat 67

Bornean Bay Cat 70

Caracal..72

Chinese Desert Cat 75

Clouded Leopard 77

Eurasian Lynx...80

Fishing Cat 83

Flat-Headed Cat..85

Jungle Cat 87

Marbled Cat...90

Pallas's Cat 93

Rusty Spotted Cat 96

CHAPTER 5 – AFRICAN CATS.............................. 99

African Golden Cat...100

African Wild Cat..101

Black-Footed Cat 103

Serval 109

CHAPTER 6 – EUROPEAN CATS................................... 114

Iberian Lynx 115

CHAPTER 7 - CONSERVATION GROUPS......................... 118

CHAPTER 8 - KEEPING EXOTIC CATS AS PETS................. 123

Exotic Hybrids...124
     "Wild" Domestic Species... 125

Opposition to Wild Cats as Pets 126

The Matter of Hybridization 127

CLOSING THOUGHTS.. 129

FREQUENTLY ASKED QUESTIONS 131

How many types of cats exist in the world?...........................131

Are all cats' carnivores? 131

Do small cats see the world in color?.....................................132

Do small wild cats retract their claws?...................................132

How do small cats use their tails?..132

Do cats have special sense organs?..133

Can small cats swim? 133

What is the ecological importance of small cats? 134

RELEVANT WEBSITES.. 135

APPENDIX I - THE JAGUAR 136

The Jaguar's Habitat 137

Diet..138

Cycle of Activity 139

Physical Characteristics 139
    Movement 140

Social Behavior 141
    Communication.. 141

Mating and Reproduction...142

Relationship with Other Felids...142

Predators..143

Jaguars in Captivity...143

WORKS CITED.. 144

PHOTOGRAPHS 145

GLOSSARY 157

INDEX.. 161

Chapter 1 – Ocelot and Margay: Kindred Cats

All of the felid groups living on the earth today were genetically established 10.8 to 6.2 million years ago. The common ancestor of the Ocelot and Margay traveled from Asia to North America 8 - 9 million years ago; then made his way down into South America.

Ocelots as a distinct species diverged between 8 and 2.9 million years ago. With only minimal variation, Ocelots have stayed in the region of their origin for millions of years. The Ocelot and Margay are more related to one another than they are to other felids. The two cats present a fascinating contrast in their habitats and hunting styles. More detailed research is readily available on the Ocelot and Margay, offering insight into the specialized niches and small cats occupy in select ecosystems.

The Ocelot: A Terrestrial Cat

When the ancient Aztecs of Mesoamerica gazed into the night sky, the constellation we call the Big Dipper was, for them, the god Tezcatlipoca. He took the form of the Ocelot, or, in the Nahuatl language, "tlalocelot" the "tiger of the field."

In Aztec mythology, Quetzalcoatl cast Tezcatlipoca, the god of the night, into the waters to pave the way for the dawn of Aztec civilization. After his fall from power, Tezcatlipoca became an Ocelot, an animal revered for its beauty and skill as a hunter.

The spotted cats appear in the mythology and symbolism of other Native American cultures. At the Hopewell Mound in Ross County, Ohio, there is an image of an Ocelot carved in human bone dating to the period 1400 - 1500.

The Ocelot's Habitat

Five hundred years ago, spotted cats that may have been the common ancestor of both the Ocelot and the Margay ranged across the southeastern United States. Today, however, only small isolated populations of the Ocelot retain a tenuous presence in far South Texas.

The cats are found in dense cover in humid tropical rainforests or dry, semi-desert scrubland. A single individual stakes out a territorial range of 1 - 4 square miles / 2.6 - 10.35 square kilometers.

Physical Characteristics

Although a lordly presence at his own level of the food chain, the Ocelot, at just 24 - 35 lbs. (11 - 16 kg) is rightfully wary of Pumas and Jaguars at 115 - 220 lbs. (53 - 100kg) and 124 - 211 lbs. (56 - 96 kg) respectively.

An Ocelot's body length ranges from 27.6 - 39.4 inches / 70-100 cm with the tail at 10.6 - 17.7 inches / 27 - 45 cm. Adults stand 15.7 - 19.7 inches / 40 – 50 cm at the shoulder. Females are smaller and lighter than males.

An Ocelot's short, sleek fur is pale cream to reddish gray with rich markings running the length of the body that may be open blotches, streaks, or rosettes with centers of russet brown.

The short, close fur turns forward at the back of the neck. On the underside, the animals are snowy white with tiny black stripes and spots.

No two Ocelots have the same markings, and the colors and patterns differ on the right and left side of each animal. Their coats are as distinctive as fingerprints. There are one or two stripes on the inside of the legs, and black rings and bars encircle the tail.

Although Ocelots are small, they have powerful mouths set with 30 sharp teeth. Their bite force quotient (BFQ) is almost twice that of a house cat and is roughly equal to that of a domestic dog:

Domestic house cat BFQ 58

Ocelot BFQ 113.8

Domestic dog BFQ 117

Jaguar BFQ 137

The Ocelot's eyes are dark brown in natural light, but golden in artificial light, set in white patches and dramatically highlighted in black edging.

The face forms an elongated triangle from the rounded ears down to the slightly pointed muzzle, which is also cream to white around the pink nose. The backs of the ears are black, with a central white spot.

Well-proportioned and compact, the Ocelot is nonetheless muscular and powerful, standing on broad, short feet. The front paws are larger than the rear and have five digits while those in back have four. Unlike domestic cats that have 8 teats, female Ocelots have only four.

There are ten sub-species:

- *Leopardus pardalis pardalis*, Amazon Rainforest

- *Leopardus pardalis aequatorialis*, Northern Andes and Central America

- *Leopardus pardalis albescens*, Eastern Mexico and Southern Texas

- *Leopardus pardalis melanurus*, Venezuela, Guyana, and Trinidad

- *Leopardus pardalis mitis*, Argentina and Paraguay

- *Leopardus pardalis nelsoni*, Southwestern Mexico

- *Leopardus pardalis pseudopardalis*, Colombia

- *Leopardus pardalis puseaus*, Ecuador

- *Leopardus pardalis sonoriensis*, Northwestern Mexico and Southern Arizona

- *Leopardus pardalis steinbachi*, Bolivia

The Ocelot goes by many names including: ozelot, tigrillo, ocelote, gato onza, tirica, cunaguaro, tigrezillo, gato bueno, maracaju-acu, gato mourisco, jaguatirica, gato maracaja, manigordo, yagua-tirica, gato tigre, tigre chico, and tigrillo.

Movement

The Ocelot is a deliberate and steady hunter, walking at a rate of approximately 0.2 mph (0.3 kph). When on territorial patrol, males will speed up to 0.5 - 0.9 mph (0.8 - 1.4 kph).

They are expert and powerful climbers, often preferring to rest from a vantage point in the trees. An Ocelot will avoid water as much as possible, but if there is no other choice, he is an excellent swimmer.

Diet

In his tastes and according to availability, the Ocelot is a generalist predator hunting on the ground and in the trees. He prefers small mammals weighing less than 2 lbs. (0.9 kg), but he can eat larger rodents like the agouti (5.3 - 13.2 lbs. / 2.4 - 6 kg) and the paca (13 - 31 lbs. / 6 - 14 kg.) Ocelots will also hunt lizards, snakes, armadillos, sloths, opossums, monkeys, and even small deer.

Since these cats have no fear of the water, they will even snag the occasional fish or crustacean including land crabs. They have two hunting styles. Either sitting and waiting immobile in a spot for as much as an hour, or slowly walking trails scanning for prey.

Analyses of the scat left by Ocelots shows a diet comprised mainly of small rodents (65%) with:

18% reptiles

7% crustaceans and fish (where available)

6% medium-sized mammals

4% birds

If the Ocelot cannot eat his kill in one feeding, he hides the carcass and will return the next night.

Cycle of Activity

Although principally a nocturnal and solitary hunter, an Ocelot adjusts his schedule to meet the habits of the available food supply. The spotted coat provides the cat excellent cover in thick brush and mottled sunlight, but the species prefers to be active at night and during periods of low light.

After peaks of activity at dusk and dawn, the Ocelot prefers to rest from first light into late afternoon. It is not unusual, however, for individuals to exhibit greater daytime activity on rainy or overcast days.

This behavior is not without exception, however. Within his home range of 1 - 4 square miles/2.6 - 10.35 square kilometers, an Ocelot will exhibit unpredictable movement patterns. Researchers have tracked solitary cats that walk for 12 hours without rest and others that spend more than a day in one place.

The amount of available moonlight has no effect on the amount of time an Ocelot forages, but the cat may shift where he hunts. For instance, if he's going after small rodents that typically avoid being out in the open under a full moon, the Ocelot will concentrate his efforts in denser vegetation.

This adaptive behavior is not seen in larger felids in the same regions like Puma and Jaguar, but the Ocelot is keenly aware of the presence of these bigger cats if they are in the neighborhood. Consequently, he'll stay out of well-lit areas for fear of becoming prey himself.

While neither the Jaguar nor the Puma is known to actively hunt these cats, the survival instinct of the smaller species tells them to stay out of the way of their larger relatives. The fact that these species also seek different types of game is helpful in avoiding potentially fatal confrontations.

Nursing females will, as circumstances and safety allow, increase their levels of activity to as much as 23-hours a day to ensure they can produce enough milk to feed their offspring.

In captivity, Ocelots become much less active and readily acclimate to two set periods of activity in the morning and evening, timed with the feedings offered to them by their captors.

It would seem that when the survival imperative is removed, an Ocelot can be as indolent as any snoozing house cat! Some captive cats do, however, show about half an hour of pacing behavior (perhaps impatience) before their food is set out.

Social Behavior

The Ocelot is a solitary hunter, but not an antisocial cat. Non-breeding males and females have been observed associating, and even after young cats become independent, they stay near their parents. Researchers have determined that when at rest, adult Ocelots stay .4-.8 miles apart (600-1200 meters.)

In any regional population of Ocelots, there are always transient and non-breeding individuals. Both males and females mark off territories and paths as their own and patrol those boundaries.

The density of available prey determines the size of one cat's space. In the rainforests of Peru, for instance, Ocelots maintain very small home ranges thanks to the high availability of food. During drought conditions, however, some Ocelots have been found to roam over as much as 34.8 square miles (90.5 km sq.)

In their interaction with one another, Ocelots have a calm and docile disposition. It is rare for males to show any aggression toward newborn kittens. The young cats play frequently with one another, and adults will play with the kittens as well.

Communication

To mark the boundaries of their territory, Ocelots spray vegetation with urine and leave feces in prominent locations. They amplify their scent signal by rubbing their anal glands on the ground and also claw at logs.

Ocelot vocalizations are frequently described as a "mutter" that becomes a "chuckle" when the cat is excited. During courtship and mating they yowl.

Their threat posture is typical of felids: arched back, stiff legs and tail raised at the root but held straight down.

Mating and Reproduction

Ocelots mate annually, and have been successfully bred in captivity. When a male is interested in a female, he follows her making soft calls that sound like "ka, ka."

She will rebuff his advances for three days before beginning to answer him with a loud, engine-like growl. The two cats rub cheeks, shoulders, and flanks, and pounce together playfully before copulating.

After a gestation period of approximately 85 days, females deliver 1-2 kittens. On rare occasions, a litter may contain as many as four offspring.

Females create well-protected dens buried in dense foliage or in a secluded spot like a rocky outcropping. The tiny kittens are born with their eyes closed. They are helpless and need the protection the den offers for several weeks.

Developmental milestones include:

14 days - eyes open

21 days - begin to walk

60 days - begin to take solid food*

* Even when they begin to eat solids, Ocelot kittens continue to nurse for six months.

It is common for Ocelot mothers to move their babies if they feel that their den location is compromised in some way. Males do not help care for the litter.

When Ocelot kittens are born, they have blue eyes. By age three months, the eyes change color. This is the stage of life when the young Ocelots are ready to begin to hunt with their mothers. They remain dependent on her for several more months, and stay with her for a full year.

Ocelots reach their full adult weight at 24 months. Females are capable of reproducing at age 18 - 22 months. Males reach sexual maturity at 2.5 years.

Relationship with Other Felids

Ocelots live in close proximity to other smaller cats including the Margay, (*Leopardus Wiedii*), Jaguarundi (*Puma yagouaroundi*), Pampas Cat (*Leopardus pajeros*), and Geoffroy's Cat (*Leopardus geoffroy*).

As the largest of the small spotted cats, Ocelots can negatively affect the numbers of their smaller neighbors. The more Ocelots in a region, the fewer small cats will be found there since they all target essentially the same prey.

Conversely, however, larger cats like the Jaguar and mountain lion (Puma) do not negatively affect the number of Ocelots in regard to food supply. The two types of cat focus on different-sized prey.

Predators

Man poses the greatest danger to Ocelots. These beautiful

creatures were almost hunted to extinction in the 1960s and 1970s for their fur. In 1972 the Endangered Species Act banned the importation of Ocelot pelts into the United States.

Today the major threat to the cats is habitat destruction. This includes clearing for roads and other structures, slash and burn agriculture, and the prevalence of timber plantations. All destroy the dense cover Ocelots need to survive.

With conservation efforts, the species has begun to slowly rebound. Ocelots are protected throughout most of their natural range, but hunting is still legal in Peru, El Salvador, and Guyana. Sadly, even in areas where laws are in place, poaching is common.

Beyond possible predation from larger felines, Ocelots are also in danger from anacondas, boa constrictors, and harpy eagles.

Still, most Ocelots live up to 20 years in the wild. In captivity, females have reached age 28, while records show that one male died at age 23.

Ocelots in Captivity

Although Ocelots have been bred successfully in captivity, females experience long periods of ovarian inactivity. This reproductively dormant period may be due to poor husbandry, or to social conditions in zoos and wildlife preserves that are not to the cats' liking.

The first Ocelot produced by artificial insemination was

born in 2011 via a joint project undertaken by the Cincinnati Zoo and Botanical Garden and the Beardsley Zoo in Connecticut. This type of research has implications for wild populations of spotted cats as well.

Lack of genetic diversity is a leading cause of population decline in the wild. Artificial insemination programs could reverse this problem by drawing on the genetic material of cats living at a distance from one another with no need to attempt to relocate the animals.

There are approximately 106 Ocelots living in accredited zoos and facilities in North America, with a target goal of a captive population of 120 to ensure viable breeding programs.

The Margay: An Arboreal Cat

The lesser-known Margay is an equally beautiful small cat that lives in jungle environments farther to the south. The word "Margay" is the English version of the Aztec word "marguey."

The literal translation is "cat of the trees," but the Aztecs also referred to this beautiful spotted cat as the "Arc of the Arrow" in reference to its incredible agility.

They were discovered by Western scientists in 1821. The scientific name, *Leopardus wiedii*, is an homage to the German naturalist and explorer Prince Maximilian of Wied.

The Margay is often confused with the Ocelot although

these cats are smaller and leaner. Margays also have longer tails. The Margay has larger spots that are less solid with a lighter central area, and distinctive fur on the neck that seems to grow backwards.

Their eyes are darker than the Ocelot's, slanted and somewhat dreamier in appearance. This gives the Margay an expression that is both benign and oddly drowsy, yet these are alert and engaged animals.

Although completely wild, Margays are just slightly larger than domestic house cats and, when young, indistinguishable from their tame brethren. As an example, in 2011, a baby Margay was found in the suburbs of Medellin, Colombia without its mother.

The orphan was taken to the Animal Welfare Foundation where it was raised by a surrogate domestic cat mother who treated the baby as one of her own, carrying it by the scruff of the neck, bathing and nursing it side by side with her own kittens. The little Margay survived, and was ultimately returned to the wild.

The Margay's Habitat

The Margay is an arboreal animal, hunting, sleeping, and even giving birth in the trees although they may also use dens in fallen logs. Their range extends from northern Mexico across Central and into South America as far as northern Argentina and Uruguay.

The cats are found on the east side of the Andes. A single individual was recorded in Texas in 1852, but researchers do not believe an actual population is present in the United

States. There is fossil evidence, however, that Margay-like cats once roamed Florida and Georgia during the Pleistocene era, a cat from which the Ocelot may also have descended.

Margays have a strong preference for primary evergreen and deciduous forests below 4,921 feet (1500 meters). The species is intolerant of changes to the landscape caused by human settlement. They refuse to cross open country with no cover.

Their conservation status is "near threatened" as a result, and they are legally protected throughout the majority of their range.

Diet

A study conducted in Brazil found that birds constitute about 55% of a Margay's diet, with reptiles accounting for

41% (primarily lizards and frogs). Because they are so agile, the cats can capture small primates and other small animals. Margays will also eat insects, fruit, and eggs.

Margays, like many cats, use grass and other vegetation as a digestive aid. There are documented reports of Margays hunting on the ground, killing and eating guinea pigs and cane rats.

Cycle of Activity

Although little is known about the lives of wild Margays, researchers believe the cats are primarily nocturnal. They spend their days resting in trees 23 - 33 feet (7-10 meters) above ground, often amid a tangle of vines.

Unlike other Central and South American felid species, they do not alter this behavior to prevailing circumstances and are, in fact, very particular in their habitat selection and behavioral cycles.

They occupy fairly large home ranges of 4.2 - 6.2 square miles (11 - 16 km2), which they delineate with urine spraying and scratch marks on branches and on the ground.

Physical Characteristics

Margays are stunningly beautiful little cats, with a slender build and large, luminous eyes. Colors vary from tawny yellow to gray brown. Their coats are marked with rows of open rosettes and dark spots, with dramatic black lines on the head, neck, and throat.

The back of each ear is marked with a central white spot. On the underside, the fur is white, while dark rings encircle the bushy tail. The fur is soft and thick, growing reversed at the neck so that it slants forward.

The pattern variation on each Margay is like the coat of an Ocelot, completely individual and as reliable a means of identification as a fingerprint.

Both males and females are similar in size and appearance. Adults range from 18 - 31 inches / 46 – 79 cm in length, with their tail measuring an additional 9 - 10 inches / 23 - 25 cm.

Adults stand approximately 12 inches / 30 cm at the shoulder and weigh 5 - 11 lbs. / 2.3 - 4.9 kg. Life expectancy in the wild is just 10 years, but captive specimens live 20 - 24 years.

There are ten sub-species:

- *Leopardus wiedii wiedii*, Eastern and Central Brazil, Paraguay, Uruguay, and Northern Argentina

- *Leopardus wiedii amazonicus*, Western Brazil, the interior of Peru, Colombia and Venezuela

- *Leopardus wiedii boliviae*, Bolivia

- *Leopardus wiedii cooperi*, Northern Mexico

- *Leopardus wiedii glauculus*, Central Mexico

- *Leopardus wiedii nicaraguae*, Honduras, Nicaragua, and Costa Rica

- *Leopardus wiedii oaxacensis*, Southern Mexico

- *Leopardus wiedii pirrensis*, Panama, Colombia, Ecuador, and Peru

- *Leopardus wiedii salvinius*, Chiapas, Guatemala, and El Salvador

- *Leopardus wiedii yucatanicus*, Yucatán

The Margay is called by man names, including: tigrillo, gato tigre, gato pintado, tigrillito, gato montes, gato de montes, gato maracaja mirim peludo, pichigueta, caucel, burricon, mbaracaya, kuichua, chulul, huamburushu, and cunaguaro.

Movement

Margays are particularly well suited for life in the tree tops. They move with almost magical fluidity. Their paws are broad and soft with unusual mobility in the digits.

A Margay can easily hang from a tree limb by a single hind foot. In that position the cat can use its flexible ankles to turn 180 degrees outward as needed while simultaneously manipulating an object with its front paws. The Clouded Leopard (*Neofelis nebulosa*) is the only other cat with similar ankles.

Even if a Margay does lose its grip, their reflexes are so fast they quickly grab another branch and pull themselves right back up. They are superb jumpers, and have been observed in captivity leaping almost 20 feet (6 meters) straight up and almost 30 feet (9 meters) horizontally. When a Margay jumps, he flings his legs out to the side like a squirrel, enhancing the aerodynamics of his movement.

One captive Margay was observed launching himself at a horizontally strung rope 6.5 feet (2 meters away). He hit the rope with his belly region, executed a somersault to hang by his hind feet, and then dropped gracefully to the ground as if the acrobatic feat was nothing but a stroll through the park.

Margays climb with phenomenal dexterity using their long, heavy tail to balance as they move from perch to perch. When these cats do decide to descend to the ground, they walk down tree trunks head first unlike any other felid.

Social Behavior

Margays are solitary creatures for the bulk of their lives. Males stay with females after mating, but leave before the kittens are born. Kittens stay with their mothers until they are around 4 months of age, and do not reach their full adult size until 10 months. Nothing else is known about the Margay's social system, or if one even exists in the wild.

Communication

For the most part Margays use only short-range vocalizations. Females emit long, moaning calls to attract males for mating. The males respond by rapidly shaking their heads from side to side and trilling or yelping. Otherwise, the species is relatively silent. They may, however, have greater vocal abilities than previously realized.

In 2005, a group of scientists working in Brazil discovered a Margay that was imitating the call of a baby pied tamarin monkey. Although the imitation was not completely accurate, it was close enough to get the attention of adult tamarins nearby and lure them closer to the waiting Margay.

Mating and Reproduction

The species breeds year round in tropical zones, but mates seasonally from October to January in other regions. Males will leave their home ranges to track a female in heat, staying with her for the remainder of the breeding season, living and hunting together until just before the kittens are born. The male then returns to his solitary lifestyle and plays no role in rearing the young.

Females can ovulate spontaneously and typically produce litters every other year. They carry their young for 76 - 85 days and give birth to a single kitten once a year. It is extremely rare for a litter of two to be born. Margays have only one set of mammary glands and are best equipped to raise a single offspring.

Kittens weigh 3 - 6 ounces (84 - 170 grams) at birth. They open their eyes at two weeks of age and begin to eat solid food at 7 - 8 weeks. Baby Margays are much darker than adults with uniform dark spots and dark gray paws. They are fully weaned at 2 months and do not reach sexual maturity until 24 months. Infant mortality in the wild is estimated to be 50%.

Relationship with Other Felids

Much of the Margay's range overlaps that of the larger Ocelot. Margay numbers tend to be lower in areas of high Ocelot concentration, even though the two species occupy different habitat zones. The Ocelot is a terrestrial cat, while the Margay prefers an arboreal lifestyle.

Predators

Until trade restrictions in the 1980s put an end to much of the fur trade, the Margay's greatest enemy was man. The cats were the fourth most heavily exploited species for their pelts, and sadly they are still hunted illegally in many areas.

Farmers often kill the cats because they are known to raid poultry houses. Margays are also at risk of predation from larger carnivores, large birds of prey, and various constrictor snakes.

Margays in Captivity

It is much rarer for a Margay to be kept in captivity than an Ocelot, though in captivity both species become more companionable. Many Margay pairs form and maintain close social bonds, especially in cases when the male has been neutered. Such couples sleep together, share food, and groom one another.

The Margay has been somewhat difficult to breed in captivity, but in November 2014, Bioparque M'Bopicuá* in Uruguay announced that one of its resident Margays had given birth to a beautiful kitten.
*The 370 – acre/ 150-hectare Bioparque M'Bopicuá seeks to breed endangered wild fauna to be re-introduced in their natural habitats at some future date. The same facility is also working to preserve the Pampas Cat.

Given the Margay's refusal to cross open boundaries, maintaining genetic diversity in the wild is a further challenge to the ultimate survival of the species. Although Ocelots and Margays exist in the world in a very different way, they descend from a common ancestor and are often mistaken for one another.

Both are spotted cats, however, the Ocelot looks out at the world in a frank, leopard-like way. There is something dreamier and more elusive about a Margay's expression, perhaps in keeping with his refusal to leave his chosen habitat.

The pair is interesting due to their close relationship and common ancestry, but the other New World felids and their relatives around the globe really illustrate the fascinating evolutionary diversity present among wild cats. Programs of this sort may prove to be the cats' salvation.

Chapter 2 – Small South American Cats

I n addition to the Ocelot and Margay there are six South American cats of interest: the Andean Cat, Geoffroy's Cat, The Jaguarundi, the Kodkod, the Pampas Cat, and the Oncilla.

Latin America

Andean Cat

The Andean Cat (*Leopardus jacobita*) is the most threatened of all the felids in the Americas, yet very little is known about this exquisite creature. They enjoy full national protection throughout their range, but the laws are poorly enforced.

On either side of the body of the Andean Cat, brownish yellow blotches form vertical lines in the cat's plush gray fur. The appearance is one of continuous stripes, augmented by dark gray bars on the chest and forelegs. The cat's underside is pale with dark spots.

The fur on the back of the large, rounded ears is black, as is the nose. Dark bands on the legs do not form complete rings, while black bars and spots mark the feet.

Six to nine dark bands encircle the black-tipped tail, which is long and magnificent (about 70% of the body length.) Long hair on the underside makes the tail appear perfectly round.

Juveniles are lighter, and have more spots and blotches on

the body, leading them to be mistaken for the Pampas Cat (*Leopardus colocolo*). There is no different in color or markings between males and females.

This medium-sized cat measures 22.4 – 25.2 inches / 57 - 64 cm in length with a tail length of 16 - 19 inches / 41 - 48 cm. The Andean Cat stands approximately 14 inches / 36 cm high and weighs approximately 8 lbs. / 4 kg.

The Andean Cat is found in a range that includes Argentina, the Patagonian steppe, Bolivia, Chile and Peru.

They live above the timberline at elevations of as much as 13,123 feet / 400 meters in rocky, arid and semi-arid zones in the Andes. The primary vegetation there is scattered clumps of grass and dwarf shrubs amid boulders and rock piles.

Little is known about Andean Cat behavior. Most sightings have been made during the day, with observation by camera trap and radio-collared tracking of crepuscular and nocturnal activity as well.

The cats seem to adapt their behavior to that of their primary prey species. Andean Cats prefer to hunt mountain viscacha, rodents in the family *Chinchillidae* that look much like rabbits with long tails.

The Andean Cat is a solitary creature, but may be seen in pairs during mating season and with their cubs after birth. Mating season, depending on location, can occur from April through October. Nothing more is known about the reproductive habits of the species.

With so much critical data lacking, developing management and conservation plans to support the long term survival of the Andean Cat is difficult at best. The cats are suffering habitat loss as a consequence of mining and cattle grazing, and their food supply is threatened by hunting.

Andean Cats themselves are killed by local people to prevent predation of small domestic livestock even though they are revered as sacred animals in many indigenous traditions throughout the region.

Geoffroy's Cat

Although widely distributed throughout South America, Geoffroy's Cat, Geoffroy *Leopardus geoffroyi*, is another little known spotted cat. The name is an homage to the French zoologist Étienne Saint-Hilaire who traveled and studied in

South America in the 19th century. Many species in the region bear his name in their taxonomy. Modern research with the cat he "discovered" indicates Geoffroy's Cat is most closely related to the Kodkod.

In the northern part of their range, Geoffroy's Cats are brilliant ochre, lightening to a silvery gray in areas farther south. They are covered in round, black dots of roughly equal size placed equidistant from one another.

The dots form an elegant "necklace" on the chest and melt into black stripes on the crown and cheeks. The lighter underside is also marked with solid spots.

The cats stand on stout legs spotted at the toes and banded on the upper portion. The tail is about half as long as the body, ringed and tipped in black. White central spots mark the rounded black ears and the striking eyes vary in color from deepest gold to a gray-green.

In wetlands and forested areas a melanistic variety of Geoffroy's Cat is seen, which appears completely black. Altogether, there are five sub-species, typified by both color variations and physical size. The larger, paler cats live in the southernmost range, while those to the north are smaller and darker.

- *Leopardus geoffroyi geoffroyi* - Central Argentina
- *Leopardus geoffroyi euxantha* - Northern Argentina and Western Bolivia
- *Leopardus geoffroyi leucobapta* - Patagonia
- *Leopardus geoffroyi paraguae* - Paraguay, Southeastern Braxil, Uruguay, Northern Argentina

- *Leopardus geoffroyisalinarium* - Northwestern and Central Argentina

Across all variations, Geoffroy's Cat is 17 – 34.6 inches in length / 43 - 88 cm, with a height of 6 - 10 inches / 15 - 25 cm. The tail is 9 – 15.7 inches / 23 - 40 cm long. Weight varies from 4 - 17 lbs. / 1.8 - 7.8 kg. Life expectancy is 18 years.

The cats are found in marshy grasslands, pampas grasslands, arid chaco shrub woodlands, and in the alpine salt desert of northwest Argentina. Although the bulk of their range is semi-arid, Geoffroy's Cats prefer the densest vegetation available.

They can be found in Bolivia, Argentina, Paraguay, and Brazil living from sea level up to elevations of 10,827 feet (3,300 meters). Although seen in the foothills of the Patagonian Andes, they do not live in conifer forests, which are the preferred habitat of another cat, the Kodkod.

The Pampas Cat lives throughout the same region, and in southern Brazil there is population overlap with the Oncilla. Due to the similarity in these species, there have been some hybrids identified by researchers.

Although a primarily terrestrial species, Geoffroy's Cats climb well and they do spend some of their time in trees. They are such good swimmers that they are often referred to as "fishing cats," and are also called "gato de montes," or "cat of the mountains."

As an opportunistic predator, Geoffroy's Cat feeds on whatever prey is most abundant, including frogs and fish. Their diet may include rabbits, rodents, and birds according to the season and local abundance. The species is nocturnal, with peak activity in the middle of the night.

Females become sexually mature at 18 months of age, with males reaching their full reproductive capacity at 24 months. Females carry their young for 72 - 78 days, giving birth to 1 - 4 offspring in dens well protected by dense shrub or rocks. The kittens weigh 2.1 - 3.5 ounces (60 - 100 grams) at birth, and nurse for 8 - 10 weeks.

Sadly, Geoffroy's Cat pelts are the second most commonly sold internationally in the fur trade. Only the American Bobcat surpasses them. Trade restrictions passed by the European Union and local protective measures have made some progress in stemming the illegal fur trade, but hunting and poaching have still taken a heavy toll on population numbers.

Many of the cats are also illegally captured for the exotic pet trade, where they are bred with domestic cats to produce hybrids known as "Safari Cats."

Although deforestation has long been considered a loss of crucial habitat for the cats, recent studies indicate that the species adapts to and begins to use the open areas, possibly mitigating the effects of this threat.

Jaguarundi

Genetically, the Jaguarundi is not related to the other small cats indigenous to South America, but is a closer relative of the Puma. In turn, both of these species share the closest genetic similarity to the cheetah (Acinonyx jubatus) found in Africa and Iran. It's speculated that the ancient ancestor of the Jaguarundi originated in Eurasia and migrated to the Americas across the Bering Strait land bridge 16,000 years ago.

The Jaguarundi or Eyra (*Puma yagouaroundi*) is a small, odd-looking wild cat found in Central and South America. The coat is smooth, and unmarked in tones of black, brown gray, and red brown.

The cat has a long, slender body and a small, flat head. There is something otter-like in their features and expression, augmented by short, round ears and closely set small eyes. A long, tapered tail and short, thin legs complete the look.

The modern Jaguarundi stands 10 - 14 inches / 25 - 36 cm tall and has a length of 21 - 30 inches / 53 - 76 cm. The tail is 12.2 – 20.5 inches / 31 - 52 cm. The cats weigh 6.6 - 15 lbs. / 3 - 7 kg.). Jaguarundi prefer to slip into dense ground vegetation for cover, but have been observed in dry scrub, grassland, swamp, savannah woodland, and forest environments.

Territoriality varies by region and population density.

Males in Belize, for instance, maintain large territories of as much as 34 - 40 square miles / 88 - 100 km2, while females limit themselves to 5 - 8 square miles / 13 - 20 km2. There, it's estimated that 1 - 5 cats can be found per 38.6 square miles / 100 km2.

In Mexico, however, were there are 20 cats per each 38.6 square miles / 100 km2 both genders confine themselves to roughly 3.5 square miles / 9 km2 of individual territory.

Jaguarundis live in a range extending from Mexico into Central America down to Argentina and Uruguay.

Of all the small South American cats, the Jaguarundi are the most active during daylight hours, with peak activity periods in the late morning and late afternoon.

They also forage and travel in pairs, hunting primarily on the ground. Their diet is more varied than that of the other New World cats, even including fruit. The species goes up into the trees for cover and refuge as needed.

Adults use 13 distinct vocal calls to communicate with one another, especially during mating which occurs at any time of the year throughout most of the Jaguarundi's range. In the northern most areas late fall is the peak-mating season. The cats choose grassy clumps, hollow trees, and dense thickets as sites for their dens.

Females carry the young for 70 days and usually give birth to 1 - 4 kittens. The babies are born with spots that soon disappear.

By six weeks, the young are eating solid food, but they develop fairly slowly, not reaching sexual maturity for 2 - 3 years. The life expectancy for the species is 15 years.

Due to their strange appearance, there is no threat to the Jaguarundi from the fur trade although they are being affected by habitat destruction. The IUCN (The International Union for Conservation of Nature) lists them as "least concern." Also, farmers hunt the cats around settled areas due to the Jaguarundi's fondness for killing domestic poultry.

Kodkod

The Kodkod or guiña (*Leopardus guigna*) is the smallest wild cat in the western hemisphere. Along with the Black-Footed Cat (*Felis nigripes*) and the Rusty-Spotted Cat (*Prionailurus rubiginosus*), the Kodkod is also one of the smallest wild felid species in the world. There are two sub-species:

- *Leopardus guigna guigna* – Southern Chile and Argentina
- *Leopardus guigna tigrillo* – Central Chile

Although physically smaller and with a thicker tail, the Kodkod is similar in appearance to the Geoffrey's cat. Adults range in length from 14.6 - 20 inches /37 - 51 cm and weigh 2.2 - 6.6 lbs. / 1.5 - 3 kg.

The base coat varies from light gray and gray brown to buff and dusk brown. It is covered in small black spots, with a few black bands on the neck and crown of the head.

The underparts are white, as is the area around the eyes. Indistinct lines appear on the cheeks and above the eyes. The ears are rounded and large, with a central white spot on the back against blackish fur.

Unlike other cats in the region, the Kodkod has a short tail, only about a third as long as his body, roughly 7.8 – 9.8 inches / 20 - 25 cm.

There are 10 - 12 pronounced rings around the bushy tail, which ends in a black tip. The cat stands on short, sturdy legs with large feet. There are recorded instances of melanistic individuals that appear completely black.

The species is found only in Central and Southern Chile, with a few observed in adjacent regions of Argentina. (Kodkods found in central Chile are plainer with no spots on their feet while those farther south are spotted and have brighter coloration.)

The cats are also seen in the lower regions of the Patagonian Mountain Forests of Argentina. They prefer the moist mixed forests of the coastal ranges at elevation of 6,234 to 8,202 feet / 1,900 to 2,500 meters.

Researchers have discovered the cats will not cross a road unless it is covered by dark shadows cast by trees. In unpopulated areas, the Kodkod is naturally active during the day, but becomes nocturnal when living near humans. The species is terrestrial, but climbs well and shelters in trees as needed.

Only scant information is available on Kodkod reproduction. Females reach sexual maturity at 24 months and carry their young for 72 - 78 days. They give birth to 1 - 3 kittens on average. Few have been studied in captivity, and none are currently housed in zoos.

In central Chile, extant populations have been affected by the destruction of native forest land for agriculture. In 2004, it was estimated that about 2,000 Kodkods remained in the area.

In southern Chile, populations are stronger and more stable, but the cats depend on a forest environment and have little tolerance for altered habitats.

Kodkods are too small to be of use in the fur trade, but they are often caught in traps set for foxes. Habitat destruction presents the greatest threat to the Kodkod's survival, but they are also hunted by farmers as a poultry predator.

Pampas Cat

The Pampas Cat (*Leopardus colocolo*) looks like a thickset domestic cat. In the wild, there are three major concentrations that have sometimes been regarded as five separate sub-species.

- *Leopardus pajeros pajeros* - Southern Chile and throughout Argentina.
- *Leopardus pajeros crespoi* - The Eastern slope of the Andes and in northwestern Argentina.
- *Leopardus pajeros garleppi* - The Peruvian Andes
- *Leopardus pajeros steinbachi* - The Bolivian Andes
- *Leopardus pajeros thomasi* - The Ecuadoran Andes

Genetic analysis has revealed that all forms intermingle with only moderate differences resulting in the offspring.

Locally, however, the cats are referred to in the following way:

Colocolo: Chile and on the west side of the Andes

Pampas Cat: Colombia to Southern Chile, and the east side of the Andes

Pantanal Cat: Brazil, Paraguay and Uruguay.

Most individuals weigh 6.6 - 9 lbs. (3 - 4 kg). Their fur adapts to the climate, coming in thick and soft in cold regions and having a straw-like consistency in warmer areas.

Colorations are equally diverse and include yellowish white, grayish yellow, brown, gray brown, silvery gray, light gray and dark rust.

On the under parts, the cats are cream to white with brown or black spots and bands. The upper coat can be marked with red gray spots and streaks or be unmarked with only brown bands on the tail and stout legs.

When a Pampas Cat is nervous, he erects guard hairs on the neck that look like a mane standing as much as 2.8 inches / 7 cm in height. This emphasizes the broadness of the cat's head, with its short, thick muzzle and large, amber eyes.

The already alert and slightly angry expression is intensified by the upright pointed ears, which are gray black on the backside with a central silver-white spot.

The cats are 16.5 - 31 inches / 42 - 79 cm in length, with bushy tails measuring 8.6 – 12.9 inches / 22 - 33 cm. They stand 11.8 – 13.8 inches / 30 - 35 cm at the shoulder.

The Pampas Cat occupies more habitat types than any other felid in Central and South America. They can be found in: grassland, cloud forest, open woodlands, swamps, savannah, and dry thorn scrub.

The species is not present in the lowland rain forest, but they do live at elevations in the Andes as high as 16,404 feet (5000 meters) where they share a range with the Cat.

The semi-arid desert of Patagonia marks the southern extent of their range, which runs north through parts of Brazil, Paraguay, Bolivia, Chile, and Ecuador with a few low numbers in Uruguay.

The species is difficult to track since they are often mistaken for feral house cats or confused with the Andean Cat.

The Pampas Cat is terrestrial and prefers to hunt at night. In areas where they must avoid large nocturnal carnivores, however, the species becomes entirely diurnal. Though small, the Pampas Cat can kill adult goats and is expert at raiding chicken coops. They have also been known to eat carrion.

The species is solitary and largely unstudied in the wild. It is believed that females carry their young from 80 - 85 days giving birth to litters of 1 - 3 kittens. The Pampas Cat is aggressive by nature and does not respond to training even after years in captivity. They are impervious to domestication in spite of their size.

The conservation status of the Pampas Cat varies by region, but they are endangered in Peru.

The IUCN Red List describes the species as "Near Threatened," citing habitat conversion and destruction as the principle threats to their survival.

Oncilla

The Oncilla (*Leopardus tigrinus*) is smaller than the Ocelot and the Margay, with a slender build and a much narrower muzzle. While a close relative of the other two cats, the Oncilla is the baby cousin — tinier, much more environmentally threatened, and extremely elusive.

There were no pictures taken of an Oncilla in the wild before a camera trap produced an image in Brazil in 2003.

There are three recognized subspecies of Oncilla:

- *Leopardus tigrinus tigrinus*, found in eastern Venezuela, Guyana, and northeastern Brazil.
- *Leopardus tigrinus Oncilla*, found in Central America.
- *Leopardus tigrinus pardinoides*, found in western Venezuela, Colombia, Ecuador, and Peru.

The Oncilla is also known as little tiger cat, little spotted cat, tigrillo, tirica, gato tigre, gato do mato, chivi, tigrillo peludo, tigre gallinero, tigrillo chico, and tigrito.

The populations in Costa Rica and central and southern Brazil have definite differences. Scientists suggest labeling them as separate species. The two groups have lived in isolation of one another for at least 3.7 million years with no interbreeding.

The Oncilla (*Leopardus tigrinus*) lives in the mountains and rainforests of Central and South America. Active at twilight and during the night, the Oncilla hunts on the ground, but is a capable and agile climber.

Oncillas prefer altitudes as high as 14,763 feet (4,500 meters) in Colombia, Ecuador, Peru, and Brazil. Their territorial distribution runs from Costa Rica through the northern portions of Argentina.

They are seen most often in edge areas between open and closed patches of vegetation. In this type of terrain rodent activity seems to peak. For this reason, the Oncilla will hunt on the edge of human habitations in regions eschewed by larger species.

Oncillas survive on a diet of lizards, birds, eggs, small mammals, invertebrates, and tree frogs. They stalk their prey from a distance, pouncing in for the kill when the smaller creature is in range.

Only rarely will an Oncilla supplement his diet with grasses. On a whole these little cats don't feed on anything that weighs more than about 3.5 ounces (100 grams). Although Oncillas prefer to hunt at night, they will adapt to daytime activity if their primary prey is diurnal.

While bearing some resemblance to domestic cats, Oncillas are longer and lighter. Adults are 14.9 – 23.2 inches / 38 - 59 cm long with tails that are 7.8 - 16.5 inches / 20 - 42 cm in length. Weight ranges from 3.3 - 6.6 lbs. / 1.5-3 kg. In captivity, some Oncilla have lived to as much as 23 years of age.

The thick, soft coat is firm and lies close to the skin. It may be light brown to rich ochre. Irregular brown or black rosettes (open in the center) cover the back and flanks. The fur on the underside is pale with dark spots, and dark rings encircle the tail.

Bold, black ocelli cover the backs of the rounded ears set well above compelling golden or light brown eyes. The leg spots taper in size as they move down toward the paws.

When viewed in isolation, the Oncilla looks like a splashy, noticeable fellow, but this is a misconception. His coloration is perfect camouflage for the mottled sunlight on the rainforest floor.

Oncillas are agile in trees, but seem to have the same ability to walk slowly down tree trunks head first after the fashion of the Margay.

Virtually nothing is known about the social behavior of the Oncilla except that the cats are nocturnal and solitary. Adults call to one another with short gurgles, but young Oncillas will also purr.

During mating, males can become extremely aggressive toward females. The species has a gestation period of 74 - 76 days. Females give birth to litters of 1 - 3 kittens.

The babies' eyes do not open for 8 - 17 days, a lengthy period in a small cat. At roughly 21 days, the kitten's teeth erupt all at once, but the young cats don't begin to take solid food until 38 - 56 days. By three months, the mother weans her litter.

Young Oncilla do not reach sexual maturity until 2 - 2.5 years of age. The average lifespan for the species is 11 years, but some recorded specimens have lived as long as 17 years.

In Brazil, the Oncilla's native range overlaps with that of Geoffroy's Cat. Some evidence exists of hybridization between the two species.

Any population of Oncilla will be negatively affected by the presence of larger cats in the same region, especially Jaguars and Ocelots. It is a matter of some debate if the larger cats prey on the tiny animals, or if the oncilla simply relocate on their own to avoid confrontation and to make maximum use of the available food supply. Their primary enemy, however, is man. The little animals have been heavily exploited for their fur and they are often killed for preying on poultry.

The International Union for the Conservation of Nature (IUCN) classifies the Oncilla as vulnerable. Deforestation is destroying their natural habitat, while poachers kill the cats for their fur. The CITES Appendix I prohibits international commerce in Oncilla or Oncilla products. Hunting is still legal in Ecuador, Guyana, Nicaragua, and Peru.

There have been two detected instances of Oncilla hybridization, with:

Geoffroy's Cat (*Leopardus geoffroyi*) in far South America and the Pampas Cat (*Leopardus pajeros*) in Central Brazil

Only a few zoos in North America, South America, and Europe keep Oncillas. In captivity the species has a high infant mortality rate.

Chapter 3 – North American Cats

There are three North American Cats. Of these, the Mountain Lion or Puma, and the Bobcat are the most widely distributed. The Canadian Lynx is the most unique of the three cats with a heavy dependence on specific habitat and food sources.

Puma

The cat referred to so far in this text as the Puma (*Puma concolor*) is known by many names because his range is the largest of any New World cat. Thirty subspecies of Puma live in a geographical swath that extends from the Yukon to the tip of South America.

Recent DNA analysis suggest that the number of subspecies should be reduced to six.

- *Puma concolor cabrerae* - Argentina

- *Puma concolor costaricensis* - Costa Rica

- *Puma concolor anthonyi* - eastern South America

- *Puma concolor couguar* - North America

- *Puma concolor concolor* - northern South America

- *Puma concolor puma* - southern South America

In Latin America, they are most commonly called the Puma, and in North America the Cougar or Mountain Lion. Other names for the cats include Florida Panther, Painter, Mexican Lion, Catamount, and Red Tiger.

(In his book *Cougar: The American Lion*, Kevin Hansen says there are more than 80 names for the species.)

The cats figure heavily in the mythology of Native American cultures. The ancient Peruvian city of Cuzco was designed in the shape of a Puma, while the Cochiti Indians in New Mexico carved life-sized statues of the cats. The tribes of the Great Lakes regions where the cats once roamed thought the lashing of the Puma's tail created waves and storms.

In Appalachia, where the Puma is known as the catamount, the cat's scream is the stuff of legends and their presence is interwoven in the lyrics of the area's famous bluegrass music. The opening verse of the song "Brown Mountain Light," for instance begins, "Way up on old Linville Mountain where the bear and the catamount reign."

Although the Jaguar is the largest of the New World cats, there is something unusually powerful in the gaze of the Puma, a look that led Christopher Columbus to liken them to the lions of the Old World, lordly kings in their realm.

Part of the Puma's folkloric quality lies in his sheer diversity. The species can be found in grasslands, swamps, semi-deserts, and coniferous, deciduous, and tropical forests.

The cats live at sea level up to an altitude of 14,764 feet / 4,500 meters. Consequently, they have an unusually high tolerance for varying environmental conditions and may migrate seasonally with their prey.

A stalking hunter, the Puma leaps on the back of its victim at the end of a short, swift chase. If the kill is large, the cat will cover it with dirt and plant matter, returning frequently to feed until the carcass is exhausted. Only rarely will a Puma eat from a carcass killed by another animal.

The Cougar is an indiscriminate carnivore. Along the western coast of Canada the cats will eat marine mammals, but their preference is for deer, which constitutes about 60-80% of their food supply. In tropical areas the cats rely more on small-medium sized prey. In Chile, for instance, the hare makes up 96% of the Puma's food intake.

Pumas, like many cats, are crepuscular, with peaks of activity at dawn and dusk. They travel and hunt at night, and alter their activity patterns to match the behavior of their prey.

A major danger to Puma populations has a direct relationship to this cycle of activity. Because the cats travel at night, cars and trucks often strike and kill Pumas crossing highways.

A large part of conservation efforts in heavily populated regions involves creating adequate underpasses so the cats can travel safely without being endangered by motor vehicle traffic.

Thanks to the Puma's extensive range, coat colors seen in this species range from a sandy, buff brown through red tones into slate or silver gray.

The puma occupies a rather strange niche in modern American folklore. "Cryptozoology" is the supposed study of animals whose existence or survival has not been proven or substantiated. One such class of animals is referred to as Phantom Black Cats or Alien Big Cats.

In spite of the numerous reports of such creatures existing, and the assertion that they may be melanistic pumas, there is no verifiable record of any black pumas in the Americas.

The hair is coarse and short with a tendency to be darker on the back with lighter shades on the chest, belly, and inner legs. Overall, however, the appearance is of a uniform tone with no markings.

The head is relatively small in relation to the body. The muzzle is dark brown to black, accentuating the glowing quality of the eyes, which may be green gold or yellow brown. The small rounded ears are black to gray on the posterior side.

Because the Puma's front legs are shorter than his hind legs, these cats seem to move with a kind of perpetual stalking manner. They have large footpads that help them to be absolutely silent. The long, slender tail, which darkens toward the tip, serves to balance the body and darkens toward the tip.

Pumas are 39.4 – 59.1 inches / 100 - 150 cm in length with a tail length of 23.6 – 35.4 inches / 60 - 90 cm. They stand 23.6 – 29.9 inches / 60 - 76 cm and weigh 66 - 176 lbs. / 30 - 80 kg.

Throughout their range, population numbers are decreasing. Their lifespan in the wild is approximately 10 years, with captive individuals living as long as 20 years.

The Puma is a muscular and athletic cat with an impressive leaping ability, easily leaving the ground to jump 18 feet / 5.5 meters into a tree. Their running speed is approximately 50 mph / 80 kph over short distances. They are equally good climbers and strong swimmers.

Aided primarily by their acute vision, Pumas also have well developed hearing, but their sense of smell is not highly evolved.

Studies using radio telemetry collars have determined that a single Puma may maintain a range of up to 38 - 40 square miles (approximately 100 km2). In North America there will be no more than four adults in a range of that size, with 1 - 8 cats occupying the same space in South America.

The only time males and females associate is during mating, a period that can last for 9 days. Otherwise, the Puma is a solitary creature, a lifestyle common among the New World cats.

Pumas communicate visually. Males routinely leave scrapings in the soil or snow to indicate their presence. The cats use a vocabulary of growls, hisses, and whistles. They can purr, like domestic cats, and are capable of letting out with hair-raising screams, a vocalization particularly associated with estrus in females.

There is no clearly defined breeding season in most of the Cougar's range. Females are seasonally polyestrous, but only give birth every other year. In North America, most births take place in the late winter and early spring.

Litters may be as large as six cubs, but the typical litter is 2-4. Females choose to give birth in caves or rock crevices or under heavy cover in thick vegetation, perhaps making use of a hollow tree or log.

The gestation period is 80 - 96 days. At birth the cubs weigh 8 - 16 ounces / 226 - 453 grams. The babies have brown buff coats covered in dark spots. Their eyes are blue and do not change for 16 months.

The cubs open their eyes at 9 - 10 days and walk at two weeks. By six weeks of age the young cats are eating some meat, but they will continue to nurse until 3 months of age. Young Pumas remain with their mothers for 18 - 24 months and continue to travel and hunt together for a few months longer. Female Pumas reach sexual maturity at 2.5 years of age and males at three years.

In many regions of South and Central America, the Puma's range overlaps with that of the Jaguar, an arrangement that works because the two species prefer different-sized prey. When a Puma shares a range with a Jaguar, the Puma lowers his preferences and takes medium-sized to smaller animals, leaving the larger food sources to the Jaguar.

The Puma has no natural enemies and occupies the top of the food chain in his area (or shares it, if there are also Jaguars in the range.) The principle predator preying on the Puma is man who kills the cat out of fear, for sport, or to protect livestock.

It has been estimated that licensed hunters kill 2,100 Cougars each year in the United States, but that figure is misleading. Only about 3% of the American population hunts for sport. It is impossible to know how many more Pumas are killed by ranchers and unlicensed hunters.

Pumas do well in captivity and can be found living in zoos and wildlife preserves throughout the Americas. Wild numbers are declining, evening though the IUCN Red List shows the species as "least concern."

Pumas were wiped out of the eastern portion of the United States and Canada in the 18th century, with only a small population surviving in Florida today. Those cats, usually called the "Florida Panther," are critically endangered.

Increasingly Pumas are spotted on the edge of human activities, which brings them into the danger zone for death or injury by guns, poisons, traps, snares, and hunting dogs. This includes government-sanctioned predator control programs.

Throughout Latin America these cats, like the Jaguar, are shot on sight as livestock predators, and often there is a bounty on their heads.

They, like all the cats of the Americas, are in need of legal protection in designated wildlife preserves where their habitat is maintained.

Thankfully, the species is not likely to go extinct due to a thriving captive population, but their future in the wild is as questionable as that of any other felid species.

Bobcat

The Bobcat (*Lynx rufus*) ranges in size from 14 - 40 lbs. / 6.4 - 18.3 kg. The largest individual on record weighed 49 lbs. / 22.2 kg. The body length is 18.9 - 49.2 inches / 48 - 125 cm with the stubby tail adding no more than 3.5 - 7.8 inches / 9 - 20 cm. Lifespan in the wild ranges from 8 - 16 years, but an impressive 32 years in captivity.

There are thirteen recognized sub-species:

- *Lynx rufus rufus* – Eastern and Midwestern United States

- *Lynx rufus gigas* – Northern New York into Novia Scotia and New Brunswick

- *Lynx rufus floridanus* – Southeastern United States inland to the Mississippi Valley extending to parts of Missouri and Illinois

- *Lynx rufus superiorensis* – The area around the western Great Lakes including portions of Michigan, Wisconsin, southern Ontario, and Minnesota

- *Lynx rufus baileyi* – Southwestern United States and Northwestern Mexico

- *Lynx rufus californicus* – California west of the Sierra Nevada Mountains

- *Lynx rufus mohavensis* – The Mohave Desert in California

- *Lynx rufus escuinipae* – Central Mexico into the west coast of southern Sonora

- *Lynx rufus fasciatus* – Oregon, Washington west of the Cascade Range, northwestern California, and southwestern British Columbia

- *Lynx rufus oaxacensis* – Oaxaca in Mexico

- *Lynx rufus pallescens* – Western Louisiana, Texas, parts of Oklahoma, south into Northern Mexico

- *Lynx rufus peninsularis* – Baja California

- *Lynx rufus texensis* – Western Louisiana, Texas, portions of Oklahoma, and into Northern Mexico

A Bobcat's coat can vary from tan to gray-brown. (In Florida, some melanistic individuals have been captured.)

Black streaks mark the body with prominent black bars on the front legs and tail. Spots cover the back and flanks, serving as superb camouflage. The pointed ears are tipped and tufted in black. Their lips, chin, and underparts are off white.

Extended hair beneath the ears and down onto the cheeks give the face an exceptionally wide appearance. The eyes are yellow with black pupils above a pinking-red nose.

Bobcats make use of all their sharp senses to aid them in their daily crepuscular hunts. They are vigilant creatures, constantly aware of their surroundings. They climb with grace and ease and can swim if necessary, but prefer to avoid the water.

The cats show a peak period of activity from three hours prior to sunset until midnight and then again from dawn until three hours after sunrise. Its nightly rambles take the average Bobcat over a habitual route of 2 - 7 miles / 3.2 - 11.3 km.

The species is highly territorial and largely solitary, but tolerant of overlapping territories. Males work out a dominance hierarchy that prevents conflict. Females, on the other hand, seem to largely ignore the "neighbors."

As a survival mechanism, a Bobcat can go for long periods with only minimal food intake. When abundant prey is available, however, they are heavy eaters and have no qualms about taking on much larger animals including deer.

The cats are stalking predators that ambush their victims with a sudden pounce or a short chase. In most cases, Bobcats prefer to take down prey in a size range of 1.5 - 12.5 lbs. / 0.68 - 5.67 kg. They have been observed to alter their hunting technique according to prey type.

Bobcats will eat rats, mice, squirrels, birds, fish, insects, rabbits, hares, and other carnivores including foxes, skunks, small dogs, and domestic cats. They will occasionally kill livestock such as sheep, goats, and poultry. The Bobcat is also considered to be a major threat to the highly endangered whooping crane.

Bobcat females are reproductively active throughout their lives, giving birth to 2 - 4 kittens on average in April or May. The gestation period is 60 - 70 days. A second litter may be born in September.

Mother Bobcats prefer caves or hollow logs for their dens. The kittens open their eyes in 9 - 10 days and begin exploring at 4 weeks. They are weaned at 2 months and travel with their mother for 3 - 5 months. Males take no part in the rearing of the young.

Canadian Lynx

The Canadian Lynx (*Lynx canadensis*) has dense, silver-brown fur with blackish markings. In the summer, the coat becomes red-brown. The cat's heavily furred ruff looks like a double-pointed beard, accentuating the animal's thick burly appearance capped by exceptionally long ear tufts. The hind legs are long, descending to broad feet well designed to travel in the deep snow. There are three known sub-species:

- *Lynx canadensis canadensis*

- *Lynx canadensis mollipilosus*

- *Lynx canadensis subsolanus**

* *Lynx canadensis subsolanus* is found on Newfoundland and is larger than the mainland cats.

The cats weigh in a range of 11 - 37 lbs. / 5 - 17 kg and are 29.9 – 41.7 inches in length / 76 - 106 cm. They stand 18.9 - 22 inches / 48 - 56 cm at the shoulder.

The Canadian Lynx is a secretive creature preferring the cover of the deep forest. They may be active at any time of the day, but are primarily nocturnal. If other predators are present in their range, like Bobcats or coyotes, the Canadian Lynx removes himself to higher altitudes or regions with deeper snow. They rarely stray more than 100 yards / 91 meters from the treeline. If necessary, they will swim.

Groups have been observed traveling together, but by nature the Canadian Lynx is a solitary animal. Individuals daily roam over a territory covering 1.5 - 3 miles (2.4 - 4.8 km). A single cat's entire home range may encompass 5.8 - 19.3 square miles / 15-50 km2.

The snowshoe hare comprises 60 - 97% of the Canadian Lynx's diet, but the cats will also eat rodents, birds, deer, and occasional carrion. The cats must consume approximately 1.3 - 2.6 lbs. / 600 - 1200 grams of food daily. They are ambush predators and will vary their tactics by prey species. The Canadian Lynx is not a fast runner and has little stamina, relying on stealth to overcome its targets.

The breeding season runs from March to May depending on location but lasts only one month. Females give birth to 1 - 4 cubs after a gestation period of 64 days. The babies weigh 6.2 - 8.3 ounces / 175 - 235 grams at birth and are grayish with black markings. Their eyes open at two weeks and they are weaned by three months. Young Canadian Lynx begin to hunt on their own at 9 months and leave their mother shortly thereafter.

The snowshoe hare comprises 60 - 97% of the Canadian Lynx's diet, but the cats will also eat rodents, birds, deer, and occasional carrion. The cats must consume approximately 1.3 - 2.6 lbs. / 600 - 1200 grams of food daily.

They are ambush predators and will vary their tactics by prey species. The Canadian Lynx is not a fast runner and has little stamina, relying on stealth to overcome its targets.

The breeding season runs from March to May depending on location but lasts only one month. Females give birth to 1 - 4 cubs after a gestation period of 64 days. The babies weigh 6.2 - 8.3 ounces / 175 - 235 grams at birth and are grayish with black markings. Their eyes open at two weeks and they are weaned by three months. Young Canadian Lynx begin to hunt on their own at 9 months and leave their mother shortly thereafter.

Although vulnerable in some localities, the current Canadian Lynx population is considered to be stable.

Chapter 4 – Asian Cats

There are twelve small cat species discussed in the following pages. Some of their ranges overlap Africa and Asia. In both regions, hybridization of small cat species is common. The following cats are among the most genetically distinct identified in South and Central Asia and China.

Asian Golden Cat

The Asian Golden Cat (*Pardofelis temminckii*) is a medium-sized wild cat indigenous to Southeastern Asia classed as "near threatened" by the IUCN. The species is named for Coenraad Jacob Temminck, a Dutch zoologist who first described the cats in 1827. It is believed that today there are fewer than 10,000 individuals living in the wild. There are three sub-species:

- *Pardofelis temminckii temminckii* – In the Himalayas, on the Southeast Asian mainland, and in Sumatra

- *Pardofelis temminckii dominicanorum* - Southeast China

- *Pardofelis temminckii tristis* - Southwest China

A well-proportioned, burly cat roughly twice the size of a domestic feline, the Asian Golden Cat has a striking golden coat. The deep colors fade to white on the underside and can vary in tone from pale cinnamon through red and golden brown hues to brown and black. Both spots and stripes may be present in the coat and there are white and black lines on the cheeks running of the top of the head.

The average body length is 26 – 41.3 inches / 66 - 105 cm with the tail adding 15.7 – 22.4 inches / 40 - 57 cm. The cats stand 22 inches / 56 cm at the shoulder and weigh on average 20 - 35 lbs. / 9 - 16 kg. In captivity Asian Golden Cats live upwards to 20 years.

They are found in Tibet, Nepal, Bhutan, India, Bangladesh, Myanmar, Thailand, Cambodia, Laos, Vietnam, Southern China, Malaysia, and Sumatra. The species has a preference for forests interspersed with rocky outcroppings, but are equally at home in a rainforest, subtropical evergreen, or deciduous environment. In the Himalayas, the Asian Golden Cat has been seen at altitudes of 9,800 feet / 3000 meters and above.

Asian Golden Cats are solitary and highly territorial. In radio collar studies they have shown the greatest activity levels at dawn and dusk. Males patrol territories covering 18.4 square miles / 47.7 km2, while females are content with 12.6 square miles / 32.6 km2.

Their primary prey includes rodents, hares, birds, reptiles, and small deer, but Asian Golden Cats are also capable of killing water buffalo calves. They kill with a single bite to the neck and are known to pluck birds before they feed on them.

Due to their elusive nature, little is understood about Asian

Golden Cat reproduction. Females are sexually mature at 18-24 months and come into estrus in 29 - day cycles. The gestation period is 78 - 80 days at which time 1 - 3 kittens are born weighing 7.8 - 8.8 ounces / 220-250 grams. The babies triple in size in just eight weeks.

Because the species lives in some of the most rapidly developing regions of the world, they are especially vulnerable to deforestation and loss of potential prey. They are also hunted as part of the illegal wildlife trade and indiscriminately killed as livestock predators. Although the Asian Golden Cat is protected throughout its range, enforcement is always problematic.

Bornean Bay Cat

The Bornean Bay Cat (*Pardofelis badia*) is an extremely rare creature found only on the island of Borneo. They are a forest-dependent species deeply threatened by habitat loss. In 2002 the IUCN classified the cats as endangered, projecting 20% population loss by 2020. A survey in 2007 found that only 2,500 adult Bornean Bay Cats remained on the island.

Body length averages 19.7 - 26.4 inches / 50 - 67 cm with a 11.8 - 15.7 inch / 30 - 40 cm tail. Adults weigh 6.6 - 8.8 lbs. / 3 - 4 kg. Since few living specimens have been studied, these estimates are based on only 12 cats that were examined between 1874 and 2004.

The Bornean Bay Cat's fur is chestnut colored on the top and sides with a pale underside. The tail is lighter and redder, while the head is gray-brown with two dark stripes running from the corner of each eye. The back of the head is marked with a dark "M."

Each ear is dark gray on the posterior side with a central white spot. The chin is also white and there are faint brown cheek stripes. The cats bear the greatest physical resemblance to the Jaguarundi of Central and South America.

The cats prefer to inhabit deep tropical forest, but have been seen across a range of habitat types. They are highly secretive and nocturnal, and are studied primarily by camera trap. An extensive survey conducted from 2003 - 2006 resulted in only one image of a Bay Cat in 5,034 nights of photo trapping. Virtually nothing is known about how the species hunts, feeds, interacts, or reproduces.

Caracal

The Caracal (*Caracal caracal*) is a desert-dwelling lynx found throughout Africa, Central Asia, Southwest Asia, and India. The cats are threatened in North Africa, and becoming rarer in central Asia and India, but are otherwise regarded as stable. There are eight sub-species:

- *Caracal Caracal caracal* - South Africa

- *Caracal caracal nubicus* - Nubia

- *Caracal caracal algira* - Algeria through Tunisia to Morocco

- *Caracal caracal lucani* - Angola north to the Congo River Basin

- *Caracal caracal schmitzi* - The Dead Sea through Syria and Pakistan to India

- *Caracal Caracal poecilotis* - Northern Nigeria

- *Caracal Caracal damarensis* - Southwest Africa

- *Caracal Caracal limpopoensis* - The Transvaal

A slender and long-legged cat, the Caracal is tawny grey to a reddish-sand colored although some individuals may be black. The skull is high and rounded, with an upswept appearance augmented by the cat's erect and dramatically tufted ears.

A dark line runs from the center of the forehead to a point just above the eyes, with stripes extending from above the corner of each eye down along the nose. White highlighting appears under the eyes, at the bridge of the nose, and on the whisker pads.

Males have a body length of 29.5 - 41.7 inches / 75 - 106 cm while females are 27.2 - 40.5 inches / 69 - 103 cm. Tail length varies from just 7.5 inches / 19.5 cm in small females to 13.4 inches / 34 cm in large males. Average weights are 17.6 - 44.1 lbs. / 8-20 kg in males and 15.4-35.1 lbs. / 7-15.9 kg in females.

In the wild, Caracals have an average lifespan of 6 years, but have been known to live 19 years in captivity.

Although occasionally observed traveling in pairs, the Caracal is a solitary animal. They employ an unusually

large range of vocalizations including an odd barking sound. Due to the arid nature of the lands they occupy, Caracals wander over large territories and can go for extended periods without drinking water, drawing moisture from their prey.

They are stalking predators, coming within about 16 feet / 5 meters of their target before finishing the kill with a sudden sprint. From a standing position, a caracal can easily leap 6.6 feet / 2 meters into the air to capture a bird. They prefer prey of less than 11 lbs. / 5 kg and routinely consume hyraxes, small rodents, and springhares. A Caracal can, however, kill an antelope and will occasionally take down adult gazelle.

Female Caracals copulate with several males before giving birth to 1-6 kittens after a gestation period of 69 - 81 days. They choose caves, burrows, or tree cavities for their dens. Kittens weigh 7 - 8.8 ounces / 198 - 250 grams at birth and open their eyes in 4 - 10 days. After being weaned at 10 weeks, they remain with their mother for a year.

Chinese Desert Cat

The Chinese Desert Cat (*Felis bieti*) may also be referred to as the Chinese Mountain Cat or the Chinese Steppe Cat. It is classed as "vulnerable" by the IUCN. Estimates suggest there are fewer than 10,000 adults living in the wild.

The cats have a body length of 27.2 – 33.1 inches / 69 - 84 cm with a tail length of 11.4 – 16.1 inches / 29 - 41 cm. Weights average 14 - 20 lbs. / 6.5 - 9 kg. Broad skulls, thick sand-colored fur studded with guard hairs, big feet, and bushy tail, make the cats appear much larger than they are.

The black-tipped tail, which is ringed in black stripes bears a resemblance to a raccoon, but the ears, also tipped in black, are lynx-like. Light horizontal stripes mark the face and legs, appearing as mere shadows in the fur. The underside is buff to while.

The species is found at elevations of as much as 16,400 feet / 5,000 meters and is equally at home in grasslands, meadows, shrubland and coniferous forests. In spite of the name, they are not actually inhabitants of true desert.

The Chinese Desert Cat is so elusive it was not photographed until 2007 and then only with a camera trap. The animals hunt mainly at night, going after rodents, birds, and pikas (small hare-like creatures.) In fact, the greatest threat to the survival of this species is not habitat destruction, but the organized poisoning of its prey, which not only diminishes the available food supply but also kills the Desert Cats themselves.

The breeding season occurs between January and March, with females giving birth to 2 - 4 kittens in secluded dens. This information is primarily derived from observations of six animals that were living in Chinese zoos in 2007. Very little is known about the behavior of the Chinese Desert Cat in the wild.

Clouded Leopard

The Clouded Leopard (*Neofelis nebulosa*) lives in the foothills of the Himalaya Mountains in Southeast Asia and China. The IUCN classified the species as vulnerable in 2008, with no more than 10,000 still present in the wild. Major threats include deforestation and commercial poaching. The animals are killed for their fur and for other body parts believed to have healing properties in traditional Asian medicine.

The cats prefer forest habitats and dense cover, and have

been recorded at altitudes as high as 12,200 feet / 3,720 meters.

There are three sub-species:

- *Neofelis nebulosa nebulosa* – Southern China to eastern Myanmar
- *Neofelis nebulosa macrosceloides* – Nepal to Myanmar
- *Neofelis nebulosa brachyura* – Taiwan (considered extinct since the 1990s)

Clouded Leopards have dark gray to dark ochre fur covered in a black and dark pattern of blotches. The head and ears are spotted in black. Partially broken stripes run from the corner of the eye over the check and from the mouth to the neck. Similar marks appear on the nape and shoulders.

Each shoulder bears a large blotch of dusky grey emphasized with a posterior dark stripe passing to the foreleg and then breaking into irregular spots. On the flanks the blotches are bordered with looped, irregular curves. Spots cover the legs and underparts, with pairs of irregular spots on the tail.

Males are slightly larger than females with a body length of 31.9 – 42.5 inches / 81 - 108 cm and a tail length of 29.1 – 35.8 inches / 74 - 91 cm. Females by comparison are 27.2 - 37 inches long / 69 - 94 cm with tails that are 24 – 32.3 inches / 61 - 82 cm. The cats stand 19.7 – 21.6 inches / 50 - 55 cm at the shoulder and weigh 25 - 51 lbs. / 11.5 - 23 kg.

Sometimes likened to a modern Saber Tooth Tiger, Clouded

Leopards have especially long canine teeth used to pierce their prey. They are highly talented climbers, coming down tree trunks headfirst and hanging from tree limbs by their hind paws to grasp items. The cats can also climb horizontal branches upside down with their backs toward the ground and can even jump forward from this position.

Individuals communicate with low snorts, and the leopards can also hiss, growl, moan, snort, and mew, but they cannot purr. They are solitary creatures, hunting at night and resting by day. The cats are patient predators, either waiting for prey to come to them, or stalking their victims.

The Clouded Leopard apparently eats various small mammals, ungulates, and birds, but most of this information is anecdotal. They also eat some vegetation and eggs.

Mating season occurs between December and March. The males are quite aggressive and can severely injure or kill females with bites to the neck that severe the vertebrae. After a gestation period of 93 days, females give birth to 1 - 5 cubs weighing 4.9 - 9.9 ounces / 140 - 280 grams. The babies are weaned at three months and become independent at 10 months.

Eurasian Lynx

The Eurasian Lynx (*Lynx lynx*) is found in the forests of Europe and Siberia as well as in Central and East Asia. It is also called the European Lynx, Common Lynx, Northern Lynx, Siberian Lynx, and Russian Lynx. Although classified by the IUCN as "least concern" there has been significant population reduction in Western Europe.

Described as a "medium-sized" cat, the Eurasian Lynx is the largest of the lynx species, standing 23.6 – 29.5 inches / 60 - 75 cm at the shoulder and measuring 31.5 – 51.2inches / 80 - 130 cm in length. The tail is 4.3 - 9.5 inches / 11 - 24.5 cm long. Males weigh 40 - 66 lbs. / 18 - 30 kg with females at 18 - 46 lbs. / 8 - 21 kg. In Siberia, however, some males have been reported in the 84 - 99 lb. / 38 - 45 kg range.

The cat's coat is short and reddish brown in summer, but thicker and silvery gray brown in winter. The underparts are white and black spots are present year round, but the pattern and number of spots varies greatly. Some individuals have black stripes on the forehead and back.

Although capable of numerous vocalizations, the Eurasian Lynx is mainly silent in keeping with its secretive nature. An individual can remain in an area for years and never be detected. Most "sightings" are simply an observation of tracks, scat, or the remnants of prey.

The cats live on a variety of small mammals including rabbits, hares, squirrels, rodents, and even foxes. Ungulates like roe deer, red deer, and reindeer are also on the menu, especially during winter. In the summer the Eurasian Lynx will also kill domestic sheep.

The Lynx is a stalking predator, but will occasionally ambush victims if the circumstances are correct. Because they have exceptionally acute vision, the cats will sometimes climb to a high point and scan the surrounding area for targets. The species is less common in areas where wolves are present.

A single Eurasian Lynx will travel 12 miles / 20 km per night patrolling and hunting, and may maintain a territory of as little as 8 square miles / 20 km2 up to 174 square miles / 450 km2.

Mating season lasts from January to April with females giving birth to 1-4 kittens in secluded dens lined with dry grass, feathers, and deer hair. The gestation period is 67 - 74 days.

The young cats weigh 8.5 - 15.2 ounces / 240 - 430 grams. Their eyes open at 10 - 12 days and they begin to eat solid food at 6 - 7 weeks, but are not weaned until 5 - 6 months. The young remain with their mother for 10 months.

Fishing Cat

The endangered Fishing Cat (*Prionailurus viverrinus*) is native to the wetlands of South and Southeast Asia. At roughly twice the size of a domestic cat, the Fishing Cat measures 22.4 – 30.7 inches / 57 - 78 cm in length with a tail that is 7.8 - 11.8 inches / 20 - 30 cm. Weights range from 11-35 lbs. / 5 - 16 kg. In captivity, the species lives up to 10 years.

Stocky and muscular in its build, the Fishing Cat stands on sturdy, short legs. Its fur is a lovely olive grey covered in dark spots forming horizontal streaks the length of the torso. The fur is white on the underside. The elongated face has a uniquely flat nose, with the short, rounded ears positioned well on the back of the head.

The ears are black on the back site and marked with a central white spot. A pair of dark stripes encircles the throat with 6 - 8 dark stripes leading from the eyes over the crown of the head and back to the nape. The tail is marked with black rings. Unlike other cats, the Fishing Cat's claws are not completely sheathed and his feet are partially webbed.

The solitary species hunts primarily at night and will swim for long distances under water. Females inhabit ranges covering 1.5 - 2.3 square miles / 4 - 6 km2 while males cover 6.2 - 8.5 square miles / 16 - 22 km2.

While fish is the cat's main prey, they also eat small rodents, birds, insects, amphibians, mollusks, reptiles, snakes, and some carrion. All prey is taken close to the water and the cats will dive from the bank to strike a target.

The species mates in January and February. The females construct their dens in dense reed thickets and give birth to 2 - 3 kittens after a gestation period of 63 - 70 days. The babies weigh about 6 ounces / 170 grams at birth and are playing in the water and taking solid food at two months. By six months the kittens are fully weaned.

The Fishing Cat's dependence on wetlands represents his greatest conservation challenge and they suffer equally from over-exploitation of local fish populations.

The American Association of Zoos and Aquariums and the European Association of Zoos and Aquariums have established programs in an effort to create a viable breeding population in captivity.

Flat-Headed Cat

The Flat-Headed Cat (*Prionailurus planiceps*) is an
endangered species found in the wetlands of Sumatra,
Borneo, and on the Thai-Malay Peninsula. There are fewer
than 2,500 individuals left in the wild with no single
population containing more than 250 adults. The cats are
extremely rare in captivity with only ten known to exist in
zoos in Malaysia and Thailand. Two of those cats lived to
14 years of age.

The Flat-Headed Cat is aptly named for the distinct cranial
depression that extends along the nose to the muzzle,
which has laterally distended sides. The effect is oddly
cylindrical, causing the distance between the eyes and the
rounded ears to be much greater than what would be
perceived as "normal." It has a head-and-body length of
16.1 to 19.7 inches / 41 to 50 cm and a short tail of 5.1 to 5.9
inches / 13 to 15 cm. It weighs 3.3 to 5.5 lbs. / 1.5 to 2.5 kg.

The unusual appearance is accentuated by the forward position of the eyes, which are quite close together. This arrangement does, however, give the Flat-Headed Cat much better stereoscopic vision.

The body is slender with delicate and elongated extremities, covered in dark brown to red fur with a mottled white underbelly. The face is lighter with white on the chin and muzzle. Buff streaks run on either side of the nose.

The cats have canine teeth twice as long as what would be seen in other cats of comparable size. The teeth and powerful jaws are well adapted to grasp slippery prey. The claws can be only partially retracted, with two-third their length normally exposed. Partial webbing between the toes creates better traction in mud.

The species is presumed to be solitary and nocturnal, although in captivity they have been noted to exhibit more crepuscular behavior. Flat-Headed Cats wash their prey like raccoons and will submerge their heads in water to catch fish, which they will carry away from the bank to eat. It is believed the cats also eat frogs, crustaceans, and rats.

Vocally, the Flat-Headed Cat makes the same range of noises as domestic cats including purring. Little is known about their reproductive habits, but captive individuals display a gestation period of 56 days. Only three litters have been recorded in zoos, with 1 - 2 kittens in each.

Like the Fishing Cat, the Flat-Headed Cat faces potential extinction from wetland and lowland habitat destruction as well as degradation of its food supply.

Jungle Cat

The Jungle Cat (*Felis chaus*) is native to Egypt, the Middle East, Asia and Southern China extending east into Southeast and Central Asia. Due to high population numbers in India, the IUCN lists the species as "least concern."

In body conformation, the Jungle Cat resembles a small lynx. The fur ranges from yellow-gray to red-brown and tawny gray. All shades show black ticking. Kittens are marked with vertical bars that disappear by adulthood. The muzzle and underside on adults are paler, but overall the appearance is one of uniform color.

Body length measures 19.7 - 37 inches / 50 - 94 cm with tails that are 7.8 - 12.2 inches / 20 - 31 cm in length. They stand 14.2 inches / 36 cm at the shoulder and weigh 6.6 - 35.3 lbs. / 3 - 16 kg. In captivity, their lifespan is 10 - 12 years.

The skull is distinguished by a broad zygomatic arch making the head appear unusually round. Broad-based long ears pointed and tufted at the end sit high on the head. Claws of equal length on the front and hind legs equip these cats for particularly adept climbing.

In spite of their name, this species is not found in the rainforest, but rather on savannas, dry forests, and in lowland reed beds. They are reasonably adaptable, but prefer the wetlands and are intolerant of cold climates. Jungle Cats have been seen at altitudes as high as 8,000 feet / 2,400 meter in the Himalayas.

There are nine sub-species:

- *Felis chaus affinis* – Himalayas from Kashmir and Nepal to Sikkim and Yunnan

- *Felis chaus kutas* - Bengal west to Kutch

- Felis chaus nilotica - Egypt

- *Felis chaus furax* - Palestine, Israel, southern Syria, and Iraq

- *Felis chaus maimanah* - Afghanistan and south of the Amu Darya River

- *Felis chaus fulvidina* – Southeast Asia from Myanmar and Thailand to Laos, Cambodia and Vietnam

- *Felis chaus prateri* – Western India and Sindh

- *Felis chaus kelaarti* - Sri Lanka and southern India south of the Kistna River

- *Felis chaus oxiana* - Amu Darya River, Vakhsh River, Gissar Valley

Like most cats, the Jungle Cat is a solitary species, but they are less nocturnal than most other felids. When cold, they find a sunny spot and stay in it as long as possible. The cats travel 1.9-3.7 miles / 3-6 km per day / night hunting rodents, small mammals, amphibians, reptiles, and juvenile wild pigs. If they are near poultry houses, the Jungle Cat is an efficient raider.

The species will swim to escape danger and to hide their scent trail. They will also dive to catch fish. As ambush predators, they can leap high in the air to catch birds and can pursue prey over a short distance at a speed of 20 mph / 32 km.

Major predators of the Jungle Cat include jackals, crocodiles, wolves, bears, and larger felines. Though small, the Jungle Cat is not timid, and will stand up to its attackers, even roaring. Most of this threat display behavior is intended purely to intimidate the attacker and buy the cat time to escape, although the Jungle Cat will jump on an opponent and claw viciously.

Females give birth between December and June, sometimes producing two litters in a year. The kittens are born after a 63 - 66 day gestation period and weigh 1.5 - 5.6 ounces / 43 - 160 grams. The babies open their eyes at roughly two weeks and are weaned at three months, hunting on their own at six months, and leaving their mother at 8 - 9 months.

Although resistant to domestication, the Jungle Cat has been hybridized with domestic cats to produce at least two breeds, the Chausie and the Jungle Bob.

Marbled Cat

Genetic analysis indicates that the Marbled Cat (*Pardofelis marmorata*), a native of South and Southeast Asia, is a close relative of the Asian Golden Cat and the Bornean Bay Cat. The species weighs 4.4 - 11 lbs. / 2 - 5 kg on average and is 17.7 – 24.4 inches / 45 - 62 cm in length, with a 13.8 – 21.6 inch / 35 - 55 cm tail. In captivity, their lifespan is approximately 12 years.

Their coat is dense and plush with dark markings on a grayish to yellow brown coat that can also exhibit ochre or red tones. The spots on the forehead and crown of the head merge at the neck to form narrow longitudinal stripes that become more irregular as they pass over the back.

Dark-edged, irregular blotches decorate the back and flanks, with black dots on the legs and underparts. Black spots and rings also appear on the tail.

Once thought to be more closely related to the world's big cats, the little Marbled Cat has interesting adaptations, including quite large canine teeth and very large feet. The cats strike a characteristic arched position when standing or resting as if they're always ready for a fight.

There are two sub-species:

- *Pardofelis marmorata marmorata* – Malay Peninsula, Sumatra, and Borneo

- *Pardofelis marmorata charltoni* – Myanmar, Sikkim, Darjeeling, Nepal

The first radio-tracked study of a Marbled Cat in 2000 found the species to be predictably crepuscular and nocturnal, covering a home range of approximately 2.2 square miles / 5.8 km2 at a maximum elevation of 3,900 feet / 1,200 meters. The species' primary prey includes rodents, birds, and reptiles.

Little is known about the reproductive habits of the Marbled Cat. Some have been born in captivity after a gestation period of 66 - 82 days. The litters were comprised of 2 kittens each, weighing 2.2 - 3 ounces / 61 - 85 grams. The babies opened their eyes in 12 days and ate solid food at 2 months.

Sadly, these beautiful little creatures are taken for their skin, meat, and bones, which are used ceremonially in native religions in the area. The Marbled Cat is protected across its range and it status is considered to be "vulnerable."

Pallas's Cat

The Pallas's Cat or Manul (*Otocolobus manul*) can be found in the grasslands and mountainous steppes of Central Asia. The IUCN designated the species as "near threatened" in 2002 citing habitat degradation and a loss of prey species.

The burly and heavily furred Pallas's Cat weighs 5.5 - 9.9 lbs. / 2.5 - 4.5 kg and measures 18.1 – 25.6 inches / 46 - 65 cm in length. The tail is 8.3 - 12.2 inches / 21 - 31 cm. Covered in plush ochre fur marked with vertical dark bars, the Pallas's cat appears much larger than his actual size. In captivity, the species has been observed to live 11 years.

Black stripes cross the white cheeks beginning at the corners of each eye. White fur on the chin and throat blend into the silky grey fur of the cat's underparts.

Concentric white and dark rings extending to the forehead emphasize the pronounced roundness of the eyes in the flattened face. Thanks to exceptionally round pupils, the Pallas's Cat has a perpetually angry expression.

The jaw is much shorter than is typical among cats, causing the Pallas's cat to have fewer teeth. Although the upper premolars are not present, the canines are quite large.

The stout legs are shorter than that of other felid species and widely set, running down to large paws equipped with unusually short claws.

There are three sub-species:

- *Otocolobus manul manul* – From the Jida River to eastern Siberia

- *Otocolobus manul nigripecta* – Tibet and Indian Kashmir

- *Otocolobus manul ferruginea* – The Missanev and Kopet-Dag Mountains, Transcaspia, Turkestan, Iran, Baluchistan, Afghanistan

The solitary Pallas's Cat spends his days in caves, rock crevices, and abandoned burrows, hunting in the late afternoon. The species uses both stalking and ambush tactics to take its diurnal prey, which includes small rodents, mammals, and birds.

The short breeding season occurs in April or May. Females give birth to 2 - 6 kittens after a gestation period of 66 - 75 days in sheltered dens they line with feathers, fur, and dried vegetation.

At birth, the kittens weigh 3.2 ounces / 90 grams. Their thick baby fur is replaced with the distinctive adult coat at 2 months and the young cats start to hunt at 4 months. By six months, they have reached their full adult size.

The fur trade in China, Mongolia, and Russia has long victimized the Pallas's Cat. The animals are frequently mistaken for marmots and shot, and they fall victim to snares set for other animals as well as to predation by domestic dogs. Since their fat and organs are also used in local folk medicine, man is a further threat to their survival.

Like many such creatures, they have the protection of the letter of the law throughout their range except in Mongolia, but enforcement in such remote regions is all but impossible.

In 2010, approximately 47 Pallas's cats were living in captivity in member zoos of the Association of Zoos and Aquariums. The infant mortality rate in captive conditions is 44.9% due to their underdeveloped immune systems. In their native habitat at high altitudes they are not exposed to viruses and are thus unusually sensitive when placed in a conservation setting.

Rusty Spotted Cat

The Rusty Spotted Cat (*Prionailurus rubiginosus*), found only in India and Sri Lanka, has been listed as "vulnerable" on the IUCN Red List since 2002. It is one of the world's smallest cats, weighing just 2 - 3.5 lbs. / 0.9 - 1.6 kg. The cats have a body length of 13.8 – 18.9 inches / 35 - 48 cm with a tail measuring 5.9 - 11.8 inches / 15 - 30 cm.

A primarily gray cat with rusty spots on the back and flanks, the underbelly is white and also spotted. The thick tail is darker with indistinct spots. Six dark streaks mark each side of the head, extending over the forehead and cheeks.

The species is seen primarily in deciduous forest, scrub, and grassland, but not in evergreen forests. Their preference is for rocky areas with thick vegetation.

There are two sub-species:

- *Prionailurus rubiginosus rubiginosus* - India
- *Prionailurus rubiginosus phillipsi* – Sri Lanka

The cats are nocturnal and at least partially arboreal although they hunt on the ground. During the day they spend their time sleeping under cover and apparently take to the trees when they need to escape larger predators. They eat rodents, birds, frogs, lizards, and insects.

Females give birth to litters of 1 - 2 kittens after a gestation period of 65 - 70 days. The babies, marked with rows of black spots, weigh 2.1 - 2.7 ounces / 60 - 77 grams at birth. Little is known about how the offspring are reared, but they reach sexual maturity at 17 - 18 months of age.

The Rusty Spotted Cat is primarily threatened by habitat loss, and is only hunted to a limited degree for the fur trade or for food. In 2010, the captive population was comprised of 56 cats in eight zoos. Forty-five of the cats were living in seven zoos in Europe.

In captivity, the species is playful and affectionate, forming deep bonds with their humans, which is a significant advantage in their long-term conservation. Their lifespan in captivity is 12 years.

Chapter 5 – African Cats

At least two of the five species of African Cats described in this chapter have contributed to the evolution of the domestic cat. The Black-Footed Cat may well be the smallest Felid species known to man. The Serval has been used to create a hybrid species called the Savannah which is popularly known as a house Cheetah. Even the tiny Sand Cat is unusually exotic and thoroughly beautiful.

African Golden Cat

The medium-sized African Golden Cat (*Profelis aurata*) is indigenous to the scrub brush and dense rainforest regions of Central and West Africa. There are two sub-species:

- *Profelis aurata aurata* – Found from the Congo to Uganda

- *Profelis aurata celidogaster* – Found throughout Western Africa.

A terrestrial species related to the Caracal and Serval, the cats measure approximately 31.5 inches / 80 cm in length with tails that are 11.8 inches / 30 cm.

The African Golden Cat's fur ranges from a reddish, cinnamon brown to grey. Some individuals may be melanistic. Faded tan or black spots may or may not be present, with lighter highlighting around the eyes and on the cheeks, chin, and throat.

The tail is darker on the top and may be heavily or lightly banded or plain. A distinctive whorled ridge appears in front of the shoulders where the hair unmistakably changes direction.

The species is sturdily built with long legs and big paws, but a small head and short tail. At roughly twice the size of a domestic cat, the average weight is 12 - 35 lbs. / 5.5 - 16 kg. They stand 14.9 – 21.6 inches / 38 - 55 cm at the shoulder. In captivity the lifespan is 12 years, but is presumed to be shorter in the wild.

The African Golden Cat is both solitary and reclusive, hunting at dusk and during the night. Their diet includes birds, rodents, small monkey, small deer, antelope, and forest hogs.

The cats breed easily in captivity, with mothers giving birth to 1 - 2 kittens after a gestation period of 75 days. At birth the babies weigh 6.3 - 8.3 ounces / 180 - 235 grams and display considerable physical agility at a young age. The eyes open in a week, and the babies are weaned at 6 - 8 weeks. Females are sexually mature at 11 months, males at 18 months.

The existing world population of African Golden Cats is estimated to be 50,000.

Incredible first footage of the animal in the wild was published in January 2015.

http://www.theguardian.com/environment/2015/jan/29/first -ever-footage-african-golden-cat-sheds-light-species

African Wild Cat

The African Wild Cat (*Felis silvestris lybica*) is found across Africa and into the Arabian Peninsula in the area around the Caspian Sea. They are seen in Morocco, Algeria, Tunisia, and Libya, as well as parts of Egypt, the West African Savannas down to the Horn of Africa (Somalia, Eritrea, Ethiopia, Djibouti, and Sudan) and into South Africa.

The species was domesticated 10,000 years ago in the Middle East and are the major contributors to the gene pool of the modern domestic cat. Even today, crossing between the African Wild Cat and domestic cats are common.

The coat ranges from a reddish hue to a pale yellow or light, sandy grey. The ears are red to grey, decorated around the opening with long, light yellow hair. The stripes on the face may be black or dark ochre. There are two horizontal stripes on the cheek and four to six on the throat, with a dark stripe running along the back.

Light flanks blend into a whitish belly, decorated with pale vertical stripes that gradually break down into spots. Two dark rings encircle the forelegs while stripes decorate the hind legs. The feet are black or dark brown.

Body length varies from 18.1 - 23.6 inches / 46 - 60 cm with the tail at 9.4 - 13.4 inches / 24 - 34 cm. Average body weight is 7.1 - 9.9 lbs. / 3.2 - 4.5 kg.

The African Wild Cat slowly stalks its prey before pouncing when in range. Favored targets are rodents and small mammals, but fish, birds, reptiles, amphibians, and insects are all on the menu. A crepuscular and nocturnal predator, the cats hide in the brush by day.

Females give birth to litters of 2 - 6 kittens after a gestation period of 56 - 69 days. The babies are born during the wet season and remain with their mothers for 5 - 6 months at which time the females are once again fertile.

The species is easily tamed and often lives with farmers.

Black-Footed Cat

The Black-Footed Cat (*Felis nigripes*) is the smallest cat in Africa, and quite possibly in the world. The average body length is 14.6 – 16.9 inches / 37 - 43 cm with an additional tail length of 6.3 - 7.8 inches / 16 - 20 cm.

Females are smaller, but both genders stand only 9.8 inches / 25 cm at the shoulder. Males weigh 4.2 - 5.4 lbs. / 1.9 - 2.45 kg, while females average 2.9 - 3.6 lbs. / 1.3 - 1.65 kg. The species is endangered, and no accurate population estimate is available. In captivity, individuals live 10 years on average.

The Black-Footed Cat is found in the southern African sub-region, Nambia, Zimbabwe, and extreme southern Angola. They live in open grasslands and semi-desert environments, but not in the driest regions. There are two sub-species:

- *Felis nigripes nigripes* - Botswana, Namibia, northern South Africa
- *Felis nigripes thomasi* - southeastern South Africa

These solitary cats are nocturnal hunters, spending the daylight hours hiding in abandoned burrows or termite mounds. A poor climber, the Black-Footed Cat stays out of the trees, digging to extend the shelter they find in burrows and other holes.

They are extremely anti-social and combative when cornered. Females range over 3.9 square miles / 10 km2 in a year, while males patrol 8.5 square miles / 22 km2. A single animal may roam 5 miles / 8 km in a night looking for prey. Black-Footed Cats survive on a diet of rodents and small birds, killing the occasional hare and eating insects and spiders.

Due to high dietary energy requirements, one Black-Footed Cat may consume 14 small animals per night to get about 9 ounces / 250 grams of food. They stalk their prey, flushing animals from cover or waiting patiently outside burrows. Unlike most other small cats, the Black-Footed Cats will hide a portion of their kill and return later to feed again.

Females are sexually mature at 8 - 12 months. After a gestation period of 63 - 68 days, they give birth to 1 - 4 kittens weighing 2.1 - 3 ounces / 60 - 84 grams. The offspring walk in two weeks, take solid food in a month, and are weaned at two months. Females may have two litters per year, raising their young in a burrow. By five months of age, the kittens are independent, but stay near the mother for a year.

Sand Cat

The Sand Cat (*Felis margarita*) may also be referred to as the Sand Dune Cat. It is the only felid species to inhabit true deserts in North Africa and Southwest and Central Asia. The species has been listed as "near threatened" by the IUCN since 2002.

The cats tolerate both heat and cold exceptionally well. They are small and stocky, with short legs and a relatively long tail, which is alternately ringed in black and buff and tipped in black. Body length ranges from 15 – 20.5 inches / 39 - 52 cm while the tail is 9.1 - 12.2 inches / 23 – 31 cm. Average weights are 3 - 7.1 lbs. / 1.35 - 3.2 kg. In captivity their lifespan is 13 years. Life expectancy in the wild is unknown.

The pale ochre fur is contrasted by buff to white underparts. A darker golden stripe angles over the cheek from the outer corner of each greenish yellow eye. There are white areas on either side of the nose extending over the whisker pad. Each front leg is marked with two dark rings, one at the level of the chest, the other an inch or so lower.

The feet are heavily furred to facilitate walking on hot sand, while the opening of the ear canal is unusually large to enhance the already keen feline sense of hearing. Because the ears are low set, the head appears to be broad. This positioning, however, keeps airborne sand out of the ears and aids in prey detection.

There are four sub-species:

- *Felis margarita margarita* – Algeria south to northern Nigeria, Sinai, and Arabia

- *Felis margarita thinobius* – From the Karakum Desert to Turkmenistan to Uzbekistan

- *Felis margarita scheffeli* – The Nushki Desert of Pakistan

- *Felis margarita harrisoni* – The Arabian Peninsula

The Sand Cat is a solitary creature with a distinct way of moving. He holds his belly to the ground running quickly with occasional leaps and sudden bursts of speed up to 19 - 25 mph / 30-40 km. Although they do mark their territory with urine, they do not leave their feces exposed.

Most of the Sand Cat's vocalizations are similar to those of the domestic cat, but also include a high-pitched bark. The cats inhabit abandoned burrows, and are seasonally diurnal, sunning to stay warm. During the hot season, however, they are predictably crepuscular and nocturnal.

Preferred prey includes all available rodents, hares, small birds, lizards, snakes, and insects. The cats will dig to pull their prey from the ground, and will bury partially consumed carcasses for later consumption.

Sand Cats mate in April or May and may give birth to two litters of three kittens each year. The babies weigh 1.4 - 2.8 ounces / 39 - 80 grams and are pale yellow or reddish with spots. Within five months the kittens reach 75% of their adult size and are fully independent at one year.

The species does not reproduce well in captivity, with a 40% infant mortality rate in the first month of life. Captive specimens are also highly susceptible to respiratory infections. In May 2010 there were 29 sand cats living in institutions accredited by the Association of Zoos and Aquariums participating in a Species Survival Plan.

Sand Cats mate in April or May and may give birth to two litters of three kittens each year. The babies weigh 1.4 - 2.8 ounces / 39 - 80 grams and are pale yellow or reddish with spots. Within five months the kittens reach 75% of their adult size and are fully independent at one year.

The species does not reproduce well in captivity, with a 40% infant mortality rate in the first month of life. Captive specimens are also highly susceptible to respiratory infections. In May 2010 there were 29 sand cats living in institutions accredited by the Association of Zoos and Aquariums participating in a Species Survival Plan.

As a consequence of this research, the first in vitro fertilization and embryo transfer occurred in January 2010 at the Al Ain Zoo in the United Arab Emirates.

A litter of four kittens were born in July 2012 at the Ramat Gan Zoo in Tel Aviv under the European Endangered Species Programme.

Habitat degradation is a major threat to the survival of the Sand Cat and they are often accidentally caught in traps set for foxes and jackals. Since the cats will kill poultry, farmers may also hunt them. Domestic dogs and cats are direct competitors for prey sources and are vectors for disease transmission.

The Sand Cat is legally protected in Algeria, Iran, Israel, Kazakhstan, Mauritania, Niger, Pakistan, and Tunisia, but not in Egypt, Mali, Morocco, Oman, Saudi Arabia, and the United Arab Emirates.

Serval

The Serval (*Leptailurus serval*), a medium-sized African species is genetically most similar to the African Golden Cat and the Caracal. They are slender, tall cats with long legs, short tails, and small heads.

Body length measures 23.2 – 36.2 inches / 59 - 92 cm with the tail at 7.8 - 17.7 inches / 20 - 45 cm. At the shoulder, a Serval stands 21.2 - 26 inches / 54 - 66 cm.

Females weigh 15 - 26 lbs. / 7-12 kg with males at 20 - 40 lbs. / 9 - 18 kg. Life expectancy in the wild is 10 years and in captivity 20 years.

The Serval (*Leptailurus serval*), a medium-sized African species is genetically most similar to the African Golden Cat and the Caracal. They are slender, tall cats with long legs, short tails, and small heads.

Body length measures 23.2 – 36.2 inches / 59 - 92 cm with the tail at 7.8 - 17.7 inches / 20 - 45 cm. At the shoulder, a Serval stands 21.2 - 26 inches / 54 - 66 cm.

Females weigh 15 - 26 lbs. / 7 - 12 kg with males at 20 - 40 lbs. / 9 - 18 kg. Life expectancy in the wild is 10 years and in captivity 20 years.

There are two types of patterning present in the species. One features bold black stripes on a tawny background with 2 - 4 stripes running from the top of the head down the neck and over the back before fragmenting into a series of spots. The second pattern is more a "freckling" of spots.

Both have erect, oval ears that are black on the posterior side with a white bar. Melanistic individuals are also common.

There are 19 sub-species:

- *Leptailurus serval serval* – Cape Province
- *Leptailurus serval beirae* - Mozambique
- *Leptailurus serval brachyurus* – West Africa to Ethiopia
- *Leptailurus serval constantinus* – Algeria, Morocco, Tunisia
- *Leptailurus serval faradijus* - Africa
- *Leptailurus serval ferrarii* - Ecuador, Peru, Brazil, Chile, Paraguay, Uruguay, Argentina
- *Leptailurus serval hamiltoni* – The Eastern Transvaal
- *Leptailurus serval hindei* - Tanzania
- *Leptailurus serval kempi* - Uganda
- *Leptailurus serval kivuensis* - Congo
- *Leptailurus serval lipostictus* – Northern Angola
- *Leptailurus serval lonnbergi* – Southern Angola
- *Leptailurus serval mababiensis* – Northern Botswana
- *Leptailurus serval pantastictus* -Africa
- *Leptailurus serval phillipsi* - Africa
- *Leptailurus serval pococki* - Africa
- *Leptailurus serval robertsi* – Western Transvaal
- *Leptailurus serval tanae* – Ethiopia, Eritrea, Somalia
- *Leptailurus serval togoensis* – Togo, Benin

The Serval's toes are elongated, lending him a high degree of mobility, which serves the cats well on the savanna lands they prefer to inhabit. This adaptation, coupled with their long legs, allows the cats to leap 7 - 12 feet / 2 - 3.6 meters into the air from a sitting position and to run over short distances at speeds of 50 mph / 80 kph.

The species does need some watercourses nearby and is not found on dry steppes or in semi-desert terrain. By the same token, however, the Serval avoids dense jungle even though they are quite capable of swimming and climbing.

As a nocturnal predator, the Serval will hunt until dawn, taking rodents, small mammals, reptiles, amphibians, and insects. A single cat may travel 1.9 - 2.5 miles / 3 - 4 km per night. Females maintain a home range of 3.7 - 7.6 square miles / 9.5 - 19.8 km2, while males expand that to 4.5 - 12.2 square miles / 11.6 - 31.5 km2.

The bulk of the cat's preferred prey weighs around 7 ounces / 200 grams. They eat so quickly they often gag and regurgitate their meal and will devour small prey whole. They do, however, pluck birds by tossing the carcass into the air and thrashing its head side to side to tear out and discard mouthfuls of plumage.

The Serval is highly intelligent, demonstrates problem-solving abilities, and apparently has a sense of humor. He is, by nature, rather mischievous. Unfortunately for small prey, this translates to several minutes of toying before the cat puts an end to the "game."

Females give birth to 2 - 4 kittens after a gestation period of 66 - 77 days. Births are timed by the peak breeding period in the local rodent population.

The kittens are born in dense, sheltered locations and at weigh approximately 8.8 ounces / 250 grams at birth. They open their eyes at 9 - 13 days and eat solid food at one month. By six months they can hunt on their own, but remain with their mother for one year.

Although not a threatened species according to the IUCN, numbers have dwindled due to habitat loss, the fur trade, and the pet trade. The cats are no longer found in the Cape Province of South Africa, and are being reintroduced in some areas.

Chapter 6 – European Cats

The matter of small cats in Europe is highly confusing, with the genetic waters getting quite murky on the dividing line between wild and domestic animals. There is a small "wildcat" (*Felis silvestris*) in Europe, but it is also present in Africa, Southwest and Central Asia, India, China and Mongolia spread out over as many as 22 sub-species.

One of those sub-species, the African Wildcat (*Felis silvestris lybica*), appears elsewhere in this book. Discussing all of the wild cat species is made more difficult by the high degree of variation by geographic region. Because they are so diverse and there is so much hybridization, think of these small cats as:

Forest wild cats in the group *silvestris*

Steppe wild cats in the group *ornata-caudata*

Bay or bush wildcats in the group *ornata-lybica*

The most distinct small cat in Europe is the Iberian Lynx, a creature that is also uniquely threatened in its home range by its dependence on a single prey source.

Iberian Lynx

The critically endangered Iberian Lynx (*Lynx pardinus*) is found on the Iberian Peninsula in southwestern Europe. The species subsists on rabbit and may have been doomed to extinction by viral hemorrhagic disease (VHD), which decimated the area's population of European rabbits in 1988. In 2011, there were only 100 - 200 surviving lynx, down from a population of 4,000 in 1960.

Rabbits constitute 79 - 87% of the lynx' diet, with males eating at least one rabbit per day, while a nursing female needs three. Although the cats will eat rodents, birds, reptiles, and amphibians, they compete for such prey with the red fox, Egyptian mongoose, and other wild cats.

The cats' intolerance to dietary adaptations is not the only threat to their survival. Their preferred habitat, native scrubland, is rapidly disappearing to developments, roads, and dams. If the Iberian Lynx does die out, it will be the first feline species to become extinct since prehistoric times.

Conservationists are hard at work with captive breeding programs, reintroducing animals into the wild. In 2013, the progress of those efforts was validated when a population survey in Andalusia found 309 lynx living wild in the area. Population monitoring is ongoing, and efforts are being made to support the rabbit population in the region as well.

The Iberian Lynx is a tawny, spotted cat with a relatively short coat and the lynx trademarks: a long double "beard" and extravagantly tufted ears. They have a body length of 33.5 – 43.3 inches / 85 - 110 centimeters and a tail that measures 4.7 - 11.8 inches / 12 - 30 cm. The average male weighs 28 lbs. / 12.9 kg while females are around 21 lbs. / 9.4 kg. In the wild, the lifespan is 13 years.

A solitary species, the Siberian Lynx stalks its prey and pounces from a close distance. Adults require a minimum territory of 1.9 - 7.7 square miles / 5 - 10 km2 whose boundaries do not fluctuate over time.

Kittens are born between March and September. Young lynx weigh 7.1 - 8.8 ounces / 200 - 250 grams at birth and remain dependent on their mothers for 7 - 10 months, then stay with her until they are 20 months of age.

Siblings begin to show violence toward one another at a month to two months of age, a behavior that peaks at 45 days. During this time, however, kittens can be killed in brutal fighting. In captivity, kittens are separated until the critical two-month period has passed.

Chapter 7 - Conservation Groups

There are numerous groups working the world over to preserve wild cats, large and small, including the large and small cats of the Americas.

The following text is taken from each of the group's website and is quoted verbatim in an effort to encapsulate the organization's mission, vision, and scope.

Bordercats Working Group Homepage - "Although BWG is concerned with all bordercats, currently the group is focused on improving the long-term health and recovery of three endangered species, the Jaguar, Jaguarundi, and Ocelot in the border regions of the USA, including areas in Texas, New Mexico, Arizona and adjacent Mexican states of Coahuila, Chihuahua, Nuevo Leon, Sonora, and Tamaulipas."

See: http://webpage.pace.edu/mgrigione/BWG/index.htm

The Cat Survival Trust – "One of its main objectives is the on-site housing of an array of wild cat species for education and conservation purposes. In particular, habitat protection is a key issue and a primary philosophy of the Trust is the conservation of wild cats in the wild. The Cat Survival Trust has secured and purchased a 10,000 acre rain forest in the Province of Misiones in northeast Argentina which has now successfully acquired protected status in the form of a designated Provincial Park. Here, not only are the native wild cat species protected but more importantly, so is the entire ecosystem.

The Cat Survival Trust believes that this is the real way forward as not only is this method more cost-effective it also involves the conservation of all the flora and fauna that make up the intricate ecosystem in which the cats so critically depend on."

See: www.catsurvivaltrust.org

Cooperative Conservation America, Binational Ocelot Recovery Project - "Conservation agencies, organizations and foundations in Texas and Tamaulipas, Mexico team up with landowners to save the endangered Ocelot through incentives-based stewardship."

See:
www.cooperativeconservationamerica.org/viewproject.asp?pid=827

Felidae Conservation Fund - "Improving the state of global wild cat ecosystems through a sequence of research, education and online technologies to benefit humanity and drive meaningful change in the natural world. The Felidae organization was formed in early 2006 to advance the conservation of wild felids throughout the world. Felidae unites a critical momentum of focus, skill, and global strategic action."

See: http://FelidaeFund.org

Feline Conservation Federation - "FCF serves its members in ways that provide husbandry education, rescue funding, and conservation and research support. FCF operates a respectable accreditation and certification process to objectively verify that animal facilities are providing their felines the standards of care that they deserve."

See: http://FelineConservation.org

Friends of the Laguna Atascosa National Wildlife Refuge - "The refuge is located in deep south Texas overlooking beautiful Laguna Madre Bay with panoramic views of South Padre Island on the eastern horizon. The refuge landscape retains its historic wildness, including extensive wetlands, beaches, dunes, tidal flats, coastal prairie, savannah, brushlands and lomas." (The refuge is home to the largest surviving population of Ocelots in Texas.)

See: http://FriendsOfLagunaAtascosaNationalWildlifeRefuge.org

International Society for Endangered Cats (ISEC) - "Our Mission: To aid in the conservation of small wild cat species through education and support for scientific field research on endangered species." The International Society for Endangered Cats (ISEC) Canada was incorporated in 1990 in Calgary, Alberta.

See: http://WildCatConservation.org

The Nature Conservancy - "The Nature Conservancy is the leading conservation organization working around the world to protect ecologically important lands and waters for nature and people. We address the most pressing conservation threats at the largest scale."

See: http://nature.org

Paria Springs Ocelot Conservation Project - "Paria Springs Trust is a non-profit company whose aim is conservation and provides the "Eco" component of the Paria Springs Project, which is an ecotourism project based on the Caribbean island of Trinidad. The vision of Paria Springs Trust is the conservation of all natural habitats and wildlife in Trinidad and Tobago, with a focus on conservation of the Ocelot, our only wildcat."

See: http://PariaSprings.com

Primera Conservation - Primero Conservation is an Arizona based nonprofit corporation that works primarily in southwestern United States and northern Mexico to create a management model for natural resources and private ranchlands that will eliminate lethal predator control and compliment grass-roots social and economic development.

It brings professionals together who have particular interests in Jaguar conservation to facilitate sustainable populations and biodiversity. Biodiversity in the northern most territory of Jaguar includes sympatric mountain lion, Ocelot, black bear, Coues white-tailed deer, and collared peccary."

See: http://PrimeroConservation.org

Wild Cat Research and Conservation, The University of Arizona - Our Vision: To conserve the 36 species of wild cats, their prey, and their habitat in perpetuity and to promote vibrant human communities nested within biologically rich, life-supporting ecosystems.

See: http://UAWildcatResearch.org

Wildlife Conservation Society - "The Wildlife Conservation Society, founded in 1895, has the clear mission to save wildlife and wild places across the globe. Our story began in the early 1900's when we successfully helped the American bison recover on the Western Plains. Today, we protect many of the world's iconic creatures here and abroad, including gorillas in the Congo, tigers in India, wolverines in the Yellowstone Rockies, and ocean giants in our world's amazing seascapes."

See: http://wcs.org

You can find current contact information on the website for each of these groups along with educational materials and venues by which you can become involved in supporting their conservation efforts.

Chapter 8 - Keeping Exotic Cats as Pets

Perhaps the most famous Ocelot owner was the artist Salvador Dali, who acquired "Babou" in the 1960s. The eccentric Dali outfitted the cat with a rhinestone-studded collar and took the animal with him wherever he went. Although the Ocelot lived an opulent lifestyle, observers did remark that the animal never appeared happy, which it probably wasn't!

It cannot be denied that people have tried and will continue to try to keep exotic cats as pets. Let me be clear from the start that I do not support the practice. Keeping these cats in zoos and sanctuaries to prevent their extinction is one thing. Attempting to turn them into exotic house pets is another.

The Ocelot for instance, is an incredibly challenging pet, paying even less attention to disciplinary command than other cat species, including the very self-possessed domestic house cat. Ocelots also have a pungent odor and are capable of letting loose with a very threatening and disturbing growl.

Exotic Hybrids

The fascination people seem to have with wild-looking, spotted cats not only has extended to capturing and attempting to domesticate them, but also to various experiments with hybridization.

In the 1950s and 1960s, a Dutch cat specialist tried to crossbreed the Oncilla with the Margay, but with little success. The woman also bred domestic Abyssinian cats, and was able to produce a hybrid from an Abyssinian male and a female Oncilla.

In the same time period, a breeder in the United States attempted a Margay / Ocelot cross in the hopes of producing a cat she planned to call a "Marlot." There have also been instances of Bobcat / Ocelot hybrids, a spontaneous cross that may appear in the wild in some parts of south Texas.

"Wild" Domestic Species

There are domestic cats that have the appearance of wild spotted cats that would be far more appropriate pets, even though some of these breeds are not without their challenges. The Egyptian Mau is the only domestic cat with naturally occurring spots, and is also the oldest of all recorded cat breeds.

The Bengal is a fully domesticated cross with the Asian Leopard Cat and is one of the most widely accepted of the hybrids. Bengals were used to develop another purely domestic breed with a "wild" appearance, the Serengeti.

The Serengeti is a cross between a Bengal and an Oriental Shorthair. It is a fully domesticated cat, but through its Bengal ancestors, has "wild" blood.

The Savannah is a cross between a house cat and an African Serval cat. They are tall, slender cats with big ears and are sometimes referred to as "house cheetahs." The breed is quite large, weighing 20 - 30 lbs. (9 - 13 kg) and was developed as recently as the 1980s. In 2012, the Savannah was granted championship status by The International Cat Association, meaning they, too, are fully accepted as a domestic cat although they have a very exotic look.

The Chausie is a mix of a domestic cat with a Jungle Cat and is also quite big, weighing as much as 22 lbs. (9 kg).

The Safari is a very rare hybrid first seen in the 1970s when domestic cats were crossed with Geoffroy's Cats. Since the two species have differing numbers of chromosomes, however, the hybridization is extremely difficult with highly unpredictable results.

Opposition to Wild Cats as Pets

There are many reasons wild cats should not be kept as pets. Beyond the fact that the animals are not happy, there are other serious considerations. For one, the practice is illegal in many parts of the world. Consider the following points:

Wild cats do not make good pets. By nature they are elusive, retiring, and shy. Most are nocturnal and even when they do develop trust for their human keepers, tend to be irritable and aggressive when annoyed.

Wild cats never lose their survival instincts. No matter how "tame" you think your pet is, sooner or later, in some situation, including a bid for escape, you or some member of your family will be attacked.

Keeping a wild cat is not as simple as having a domestic cat. It is a lifetime commitment that may even require modification of your dwelling to ensure the safety of the animal and to prevent its escape.

This can involve zoning and legality issues, not to mention potential nightmare wrangles with homeowners associations and similar groups. In all of these political contests, the cat is usually the loser — often to the point of losing its life.

Keeping a wild cat in captivity removes desperately needed genetic material from the already shrinking gene pool, thus *promoting* rather than *preventing* extinction of the species.

When wild kittens are captured for sale in the pet trade, the mother cat is usually killed. This further depletes the gene pool and reduces the viable breeding population.

As the numbers of wild cats diminish, the food chain becomes disrupted, creating a domino effect that contributes to the endangerment of other species.

The Matter of Hybridization

This chapter began with a discussion of domestic cat breeds created through hybridization with wild cats. I included this information because the breeds are extant and available, but you should be aware that the practice meets with the complete disapproval of the wild cat conservation community.

Hybridization with domestic cats is as serious a threat to the integrity of the gene pool as misguided efforts to make pets of these gorgeous wild creatures.

The cats that are the product of such hybridization, especially in the first few generations of breeding, require highly specialized care from knowledgeable owners.

These cats that live in a nether world between a wild and domesticated status often suffer from being kept by people who simply do not understand them or understand how to care for them.

Every wild cat species evolved over thousands of years to occupy a unique niche in its natural environment. The idea that humans can play with that process to mix and match genes and come up with an "improved" version of the creature that can be domesticated is not only arrogant, but often doomed to failure.

Simply put, nothing that dilutes the wild gene pool in any way is good for the ultimate survival of species. The often-quoted line from the film *Jurassic Park* very much applies in this situation. "Your scientists were so preoccupied with whether or not they *could* that they didn't stop to think if they *should*."

If you want a cat as a pet, there are hundreds of thousands of beautiful creatures sitting in shelters in desperate need of a home. Take these fully domesticated felines into your family, and admire and support the wild cat species with your donation dollars and volunteer conservation efforts.

Closing Thoughts

Scientists use a term called the "observer effect." It refers to the phenomenon of being watched or observed. The idea is that the act of observation changes that which is observed. I have long hoped that simply observing what we are doing to our planet and its creatures will help us change our behavior.

The poet and author Maya Angelou said, "I did then what I knew how to do. Now that I know better, I do better." We can and must do better by all the animal species of the world, especially these lovely small cats.

Beyond the fact that they are beautiful, these species also illustrate the delicate interaction of animals and their environment. Some of these creatures are so particular about their habitat they will not cross an open area even in pursuit of a mate. This leads to a decline in genetic diversity that weakens the entire population.

Add to that the problem of poaching and the pet trade, and the lack of a vital gene pool may kill off some of these species before habitat destruction has a chance to do the deed. There may well be a time when the only place you can see an Ocelot or a Margay is in zoo or wildlife preserve. While this is far preferable to a species going extinct, it is a sad commentary on our stewardship of the planet.

There is considerable concern today about the presence of genetically modified organisms in our food supply, yet there are those people who think that capturing wild animals to create hybrid "domestic" species is a good idea.

As a great lover of cats, I do understand the pull of living with an exotic-looking feline companion, but I don't want to do that at the genetic expense of endangered feline species in the wild.

I hope you have come away from this text with both a new awareness and a new appreciation for the world's wild cat species. Each is unique and valuable.

As I said in the foreword, I was unaware of many of these species until I began my research on the Ocelot and Margay. As a cat lover, that gap in my feline knowledge bothered me, but I would have been far more bothered to discover that I was learning about species that had recently gone extinct.

Although many of these cats are endangered, all can be saved by the efforts of people genuinely interested in their conservation. If you have now joined those ranks, this text has served its purpose.

Frequently Asked Questions

As you will see, the various cats living in Central and South America, and in fact, throughout the world, share many common characteristics.

Some of the most frequently asked questions about these cats, their abilities, and behaviors include the following:

How many types of cats exist in the world?

Small cats are one of the world's most widely known and recognized mammals. All are members of the *Felidae* family. This includes the domestic cats that live in our homes. There are 37 species of cats in the *Felidae* family.

Are all cats' carnivores?

All cats are obligate meat eaters or carnivores, and evolution has uniquely designed them for a predatory way of life. They have 28-30 teeth in a foreshortened jaw equipped with simple, small incisors and upper and lower canines.

Cats use their four prominent canine teeth to penetrate the hide or skin of their prey. Often the cat will dispatch the prey with one fatal bite on the back of the neck, using the canines to separate the vertebrae and sever the spinal column.

Do small cats see the world in color?

Cats, like humans, have binocular vision, but unlike us, their vision is dichromatic not trichromatic. A feline's eyes have only the necessary structures to see blue and green light, but they cannot detect red light. In human terms, therefore, they are "color blind."

Instead, cats see much more efficiently in low light. Their eyes have more rods than cones, allowing them to function well at night and to detect movement quickly. This adaption is especially strong in the smaller felids.

Do small wild cats retract their claws?

The claws of wild cats are fully retractable, and their importance cannot be overstated. Cats use their claws for climbing, as weapons of defense, and to secure and grasp prey.

When the cat needs its claws, tendons in the paws contract, causing the terminal phalanx (last digit of the toe) to extend the claw. At the same time, a ligament attached to the claw stretches fully, ready to tighten and serve as a spring to bring the claw back into the sheath of skin.

Unlike dogs, which cannot retract their claws, a cat can move in utter silence when its claws are drawn in.

How do small cats use their tails?

It's possible to deduce many things about a cat's habits by looking at its tail. The Andean Cat is a good example. The species occupies high, treeless stretches of the Andes where they use their large, bushy tail as a scarf to cover their paws and nose when resting or sleeping.

The Margay has a long, heavy tail that works to counterbalance its agile movements through the trees. Geoffroy's Cat, on the other hand, uses its short, muscular tail as an aid when swimming, almost like a rudder.

Do cats have special sense organs?

Of course cats make use of the same five senses we have — sight, smell, sound, taste, and touch — all developed to differing degrees. Their whiskers, or vibrissae, serve as special sense organs.

The whiskers appear in rows across the cheeks in a fleshy portion of the face called the whisker pad, as well as above the eyes, below the chin, and on the "wrist."

Vibrissae are extremely sensitive to air currents or to the struggles of a prey animal. The whiskers do not have to be in contact with an object for this sensory input to be interpreted. The sensitivity of the whiskers is the secret of a blind cat's ability to navigate.

Even when robbed of its vision, a cat can "read" air currents flowing around an object in its path and avoid colliding with it. This ability, more than visual acuity, explains a cat's ability to navigate in the dark.

Can small cats swim?

All small cats, including domestic cats, swim well, but will go out of their way to avoid doing so. The exception in this group is Geoffroy's Cat, which is known as the "fishing cat." They routinely go after aquatic prey, primarily frogs and fish, and do not mind that water at all.

What is the ecological importance of small cats?

Small cats occupy an important role in the food chain. All biological organisms face limiting factors to population growth including disease and predation.

Small cats are top predators. They eat the prey that is most common and easiest to catch, thus limiting the population to the most successful members of the given group. Thus, they help to maintain higher biodiversity.

Relevant Websites

Big Cat Rescue
www.bigcatrescue.org

The Cat Survival Trust
www.catsurvivaltrust.org

Ecology of the Ocelot and Margay
www.ecology.info/ecology-Ocelot-Margay.htm

Felidae Conservation Fund
www.felidaefund.org

Feline Conservation Federation
www.felineconservation.org

The IUCN Red List: Margay
www.iucnredlist.org/details/11511/0

The IUCN Red List: Ocelot
www.iucnredlist.org/details/11509/0

The IUCN Red List: Oncilla
www.iucnredlist.org/details/11510/0

International Society for Endangered Cats
www.wildcatconservation.org

Paria Springs Eco Community Ocelot Conservation Project
http://www.pariasprings.com/events/ocelotproject.html

Viva the Ocelot
www.facebook.com/VivatheOcelot

Wildcat Sanctuary
www.wildcatsanctuary.org

Appendix I - The Jaguar

The 16th century Aztec story of the Ocelot god Tezcatlipoca seems to have been derived from earlier Toltec (c. 800 - 1000 CE) Jaguar mythology. Since both spotted cats appear in the ceremonial art of these native cultures, it's sometimes difficult to distinguish the two.

Perhaps the most telling aspect of this mythology, however, is that the creatures were seen to bring both good fortune and misery according to the dictates of the time. The cat gods were perceived to be the masters and the people their slaves.

It's easy to understand how the feline majesty and impassive stare of *Panthera onca*, the Jaguar, could be associated with such implacable control.

The Jaguar is the third-largest cat in the world after the tiger and the lion and the largest of the New World cats. Sometimes referred to as a "black leopard" if he sports a melanistic coat, the Jaguar should not be confused with *Panthera pardus*, a species found only in Africa and Asia.

Padding through the world silently on over-sized paws, the Jaguar is a study in contained power. Solidly at the top of the food chain in his range, the Jaguar's greatest threat is the ongoing challenge of sharing his world with man.

The Jaguar's Habitat

While most often associated with the deepest reaches of the tropical rainforest, Jaguars can adapt to a variety of habitats. They once roamed throughout the Americas, but are now found from extreme Southern Arizona to northern Argentina. Their habitats include:

- flooded lowland rainforests
- swampy grasslands
- evergreen forests
- arid scrub forests
- mangrove swamps

Jaguars do, however, stay as close as possible to water, typically within .3 miles (.5 km). In Costa Rica, the cats have been spotted at elevations of 12,467 feet (3,800 meters), but no higher than 8,858 feet (2,700 meters) in the Andes.

The amount of personal territory maintained by an individual Jaguar varies by region. In the Yucatan Peninsula, for instance, male Jaguars patrol 12.7 square miles (33 km2) while females limit themselves to 3.86 square miles (10 km2.)

In Brazil, however, both genders prowl about 54.8 square miles (142 km2). A male's range typically overlaps or encloses that of two females.

Diet

Jaguars hunt primarily at night, using their excellent vision to detect any one of the 85 species they are known to consume. These opportunistic predators use their equally sharp vision and teeth to stalk and ambush their targets, crushing the skulls of their prey with a single bite.

The Jaguar then drags the carcasses under cover to be

consumed at leisure, a behavior seen in many large felids. Jaguars prefer tapirs (herbivorous mammals that look like pigs), peccaries (also pig-like mammals), and deer, but they will eat almost anything they can catch. Their diet includes armadillos, capybara, squirrels, birds, and even snails.

Because the Jaguar has neither a fear of nor distaste for the water, the cats will also snatch fish, turtles, and young caiman (a creature much like a crocodile.) Similarly, the Jaguar will instantly call on his arboreal skills if a monkey or other tree-dwelling creature ventures too close to the ground.

Since cattle ranches are a major industry through much of the Jaguars' range, especially in Brazil and Venezuela, the cats can be the bane of ranchers. For this reason, Jaguars are often shot on sight to protect livestock in the area.

Cycle of Activity

Jaguars are classed as nocturnal animals, but like most species such a cut-and-dried classification doesn't do justice to the complexity of their habits. Radio telemetry studies show they will hunt during the day as the opportunity arises, and are more truly crepuscular, with peaks of activity at dawn and dusk.

Physical Characteristics

Jaguars are larger than leopards, with broader heads and muzzles, thicker legs, and a heavier frame. The irises of the cat's eyes are yellow gold or greenish yellow, glowing brightly in a face that is by turns intense or impassive. The small, rounded ears sit low on the head and feature a central white spot on the black anterior side.

Body length ranges from 43.3 – 66.9 inches / 110 - 170 cm with a tail length of 17.3 – 31.5 inches / 44 - 80 cm. Jaguars stand 26 – 29.1 inches / 66 - 74 cm, and weigh 125 - 300 lbs. (57 - 136 kg.) Population numbers are in decline and the species is considered to be "near threatened."

The Jaguar's coat is short and stiff, ranging from pale gold though yellow brown to rust red. Black spots mark the head, neck, and limbs, while dark blotches appear on the white or buff under parts.

The patterns on the shoulders, back, and flanks are rosettes with broken edges enclosing one or more dots in a field darker than that of the coat's base color.

Melanistic individuals appear to be completely black. In bright sunlight, however, all the regular markings and patterns are still present. A Jaguar's short, thick tail is completely spotted with a black tip.

Jaguars that live in forests tend to be darker, while those living in more open areas are lighter. Size also varies by location, with the biggest of these cats found in Venezuela and the Pantanal of Brazil.

In captivity, a Jaguar can live up to 22 years.

Movement

Jaguars are excellent climbers, but lack the almost preternatural agility of the leopard. They are also strong swimmers, and will cross wide streams without hesitation. They swim with their head and spine out of the water.

Eyewitness reports exist of Jaguars crossing the Panama Canal, which is 110 feet / 33.5 meters wide.

In spite of their arboreal abilities, the cats are primarily terrestrial, padding silently through the rainforests and across fields on their oversized pads. The average stride length is 19.7 inches / 50 cm.

As ambush predators, Jaguars tire quickly when moving at top speed. They prefer to walk into their range of attack and then charge for no more than 23 - 98 feet / 7 - 30 meters.

Social Behavior

The Jaguar is a solitary and territorial animal except for the time spent with the mother during the years of juvenile development. Young females remain with their mothers for 2 years, while males need 3 - 4 years to gain their full size and reach sexual maturity.

Communication

The sound most often recorded in Jaguars is a hoarse cough or bark sometimes described as a "grunt" or "snore." This is typical in both males and females and is used to maintain home range boundaries and communicate over a distance. Male vocalizations are deeper and more resounding, but easily outpaced by a female's calls during estrus. All vocalizations are instinctual not taught.

As Jaguars age, they develop a low-pitched roar, which is a consequence of the larynx shifting downward causing the vocal tract to lengthen. They also exhibit the "chuffing" common in tigers, snow leopards, and clouded leopards.

Non-verbal communication primarily involves territorial markings and includes scraping at the ground with the hind paws, scent marking, tree raking, head rubbing, and depositing urine and feces.

Mating and Reproduction

Females are capable of breeding year round. Throughout most of the range in which the Jaguar is found, there is no specific breeding season. In the far north, however, mating occurs in December and January with cubs born in April and May after a 90 - 105 day gestation period.

The young Jaguars weigh 24.69 - 31.74 ounces (700 - 900 grams). The cubs have pale bluff fur that is long and wooly. They are marked with round black facial spots and black facial lines. The babies open their eyes at 11 - 13 days and begin walking at 18 days.

By 70 days, the young cats are eating solid food and will be weaned at 4 - 5 months. The juveniles then stay with their mother until they are fully grown and sexually mature. This takes two years for females and 3 - 4 for males.

Relationship with Other Felids

Jaguars live in overlapping territories with Pumas, an arrangement that works because the two species specialize in different sized prey. Scientists theorize that the cats avoid conflict by picking preferred patches of territory and sticking to them.

Studies also indicate that the Puma, in deference to his larger neighbor, adjusts his prey preference downward, allowing the larger cat to have the bigger food animals in the area.

There are anecdotal accounts of Jaguars attacking both Pumas and Ocelots, incidents which may result from chance encounters but no reported attacks on humans. The cats will attack cattle, but tend to leave livestock alone if more aggressive water buffalo are mixed in with the herd as guard animals.

Predators

Man is the Jaguar's primary threat, both by direct hunting and by habitat destruction. The cats are also vulnerable to injury from wounds from various prey animals like peccaries, a pig-like species with tusks, and the capybara, which can deliver wicked bites with their large, dangerous teeth.

Jaguars in Captivity

Jaguars thrive in captivity to the point that only 22 of the 95 specimens currently living in the United States can be traced back to nature. Under the approved Species Survival Plan (SSP) formulated by the American Zoo and Aquarium Association (AZA), 39 zoos are part of a dedicated long-term management and conservation program for the species.

Although "near threatened," the Jaguar is not in danger of going extinct as a result of these efforts. The SSP does call, however, to raise the captive population in the U.S. from 85 to 120 individuals to ensure genetic diversity.

Works Cited

Bonar, Samantha. *Small Wildcats*. Watts Library, 2003.

Cisin, Catherine. *An Ocelot in Your Home: A Guide to the Selection, Care, and Training of Ocelots and Margays*. T.F.H. Publications, 1968.

Macdonald, David and Andrew Loveridge. *The Biology and Conservation of Wild Felids*. Oxford University Press, 2010.

Markovics, Joyce L. *Jaguarundi: Otter Cat*. America's Hidden Animal Treasures, 2012.

Merrill, Meg. *Know Your Ocelots and Margays*. The Pet Library, 1974.

Randall, Henry. *Ocelots / Ocelotes (Cats of the Wild / Felinos Salvajes)*. PowerKids Press, 2011.

Sanderson, James G. and Patrick Wilson. *Small Wild Cats: The Animal Answer Guide*. Johns Hopkins University Press, 2011.

Sunquist, Fiona and Mel Sunquist. *The Wild Cat Book: Everything You Ever Wanted to Know About Cats*. University of Chicao Press, 2014.

Wainwright, Mark and Oscar Arias. *The Mammals of Costa Rica: A Natural History and Field Guide*. Cornell University Press, 2007.

Photographs

http://commons.wikimedia.org/wiki/File%3AOcelot_in_Bul
ivia.JPG
By Ella Sanders, via Wikimedia Commons

http://commons.wikimedia.org/wiki/File%3AOcelot_(Leop
ardus_pardalis)-8.jpg
By Ana_Cotta, via Wikimedia Commons

http://commons.wikimedia.org/wiki/File%3AOcelot_01.jpg
By Danleo, via Wikimedia Commons

http://commons.wikimedia.org/wiki/File%3AMargaykat_Le
opardus_wiedii.jpg
By Malene Thyssen, via Wikimedia Commons

http://commons.wikimedia.org/wiki/File%3AMargayFourr
ure.jpg
By Abujoy, via Wikimedia Commons

http://commons.wikimedia.org/wiki/File%3AMargay.jpg
By Clément, via Wikimedia Commons

https://www.flickr.com/photos/miguelvieira/6225790697/
Miguel Vieira via flickr

http://commons.wikimedia.org/wiki/File%3AAndean_cat_1
_Jim_Sanderson.jpg
By Jim Sanderson, via Wikimedia Commons

http://commons.wikimedia.org/wiki/File%3AGeoffroy's_Cat.jpg
By Charles Barilleaux from Cincinnati, Ohio, United States of America (Geoffroy's Cat), via Wikimedia Commons

http://commons.wikimedia.org/wiki/File%3AGeoffrey'sCat2.jpg
By Greg Hume, via Wikimedia Commons

https://www.flickr.com/photos/tambako/10568663315/
Tambako The Jaguar via flickr

http://commons.wikimedia.org/wiki/File%3AJaguarundi_Zoo_Berlin.JPG
By UrLunkwill, via Wikimedia Commons

http://commons.wikimedia.org/wiki/File%3ALeopardus_gu
igna.jpeg
By Mauro Tammone, via Wikimedia Commons

http://commons.wikimedia.org/wiki/File%3AGuigna_Jim_S
anderson.jpg
By Jim Sanderson, via Wikimedia Commons

http://commons.wikimedia.org/wiki/File%3ALeopardus_pa
jeros_20101006.jpg
By ZooPro, via Wikimedia Commons

http://pixabay.com/en/puma-mountain-lion-crouching-
cougar-427276
Corinna Stoeffl via pixabay

http://commons.wikimedia.org/wiki/File%3AMountain-lion-01623.jpg
By K Fink (NPS) [Public domain], via Wikimedia Commons

http://commons.wikimedia.org/wiki/File%3ABobcat-snow-tree_-_West_Virginia_-_ForestWander.jpg
via Wikimedia Commons

http://commons.wikimedia.org/wiki/File%3ALynx_Canadensis.jpg
By Keith Williams, via Wikimedia Commons

http://commons.wikimedia.org/wiki/File%3ACanada_Lynx_(6187103428).jpg
By Denali National Park and Preserve (Canada Lynx Uploaded by AlbertHerring), via Wikimedia Commons

http://commons.wikimedia.org/wiki/File%3AAsian_Golden_cat.jpg

By Karen Stout, via Wikimedia Commons

http://commons.wikimedia.org/wiki/File%3AAsian_golden_cat_at_Edingburgh_Zoo.jpg

By Marie Hale (Flickr: Asian golden cat), via Wikimedia Commons

http://commons.wikimedia.org/wiki/File%3ABay_cat_1_Jim_Sanderson.jpg

By Jim Sanderson, via Wikimedia Commons

http://commons.wikimedia.org/wiki/File:Caracal_hunting_in_the_serengeti.jpg

By Nick and Melissa Baker

http://commons.wikimedia.org/wiki/File%3ASemi-Wild_Cat.jpg

By Steve Snodgrass from Washington DC, USA (Semi-Wild Cat) via Wikimedia Commons

http://commons.wikimedia.org/wiki/File%3AChinese_Mountain_Cat_(Felis_Bieti)_in_XiNing_Wild_Zoo.jpg

By 西宁野生动物园, via Wikimedia Commons

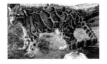

http://commons.wikimedia.org/wiki/File:Neofelis_nebulosa.jpg

Photo by Nancy Vandermey of EFBC"s Feline Conservation Center, Rosamond CA http://www.wildcatzoo.org

http://commons.wikimedia.org/wiki/File%3ALynx_Nationalpark_Bayerischer_Wald_01.jpg

By Aconcagua, via Wikimedia Commons

http://commons.wikimedia.org/wiki/File%3ALynx_lynx_po
ing.jpg
By Bernard Landgraf (User:Baerni),via Wikimedia
Commons

http://commons.wikimedia.org/wiki/File%3AFishing_Cat_(
Prionailurus_viverrinus)_3.jpg
By Cliff, via Wikimedia Commons

http://commons.wikimedia.org/wiki/File%3AFlat-
headed_cat_1_Jim_Sanderson.JPG
By Jim Sanderson, via Wikimedia Commons

http://commons.wikimedia.org/wiki/File%3AZoo_de_Pont-
Scorff_Chaus_2.JPG
By Abujoy, via Wikimedia Commons

http://commons.wikimedia.org/wiki/File%3AFelisChausMu
nsiari1.jpg
By L. Shyamal, via Wikimedia Commons

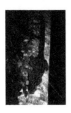

http://commons.wikimedia.org/wiki/File%3AMarbled_cat_
borneo.jpg
By Johan Embréus, via Wikimedia Commons

http://commons.wikimedia.org/wiki/File%3AManoel.jpg
By Jar0d, via Wikimedia Commons

http://commons.wikimedia.org/wiki/File%3APallas_Cat.jpg
By Keven Law, via Wikimedia Commons

http://commons.wikimedia.org/wiki/File%3ARostkatze.JPG
By UrLunkwill, via Wikimedia Commons

http://commons.wikimedia.org/wiki/File:AfricanWildCat.jp
g
African Wild Cat, photographed, by Sonelle

http://commons.wikimedia.org/wiki/File%3AFelis_nigripes
_5.JPG
By Pierre de Chabannes pour http://www.photozoo.org ,
via Wikimedia Commons

http://commons.wikimedia.org/wiki/File%3APersian_sand_
CAT.jpg
By Payman sazesh, via Wikimedia Commons

https://www.flickr.com/photos/bontempscharly/8133366989
Charles Barilleaux via flickr

http://commons.wikimedia.org/wiki/File%3AServal_in_Tanzania.jpg
By Self via Wikimedia Commons

http://pixabay.com/en/serval-small-cat-wildcat-predators-84082
Raik Thorstad via pixabay

http://commons.wikimedia.org/wiki/File%3AIberian_Lynx_full_body.JPG
By http://www.lynxexsitu.es , via Wikimedia Commons

http://commons.wikimedia.org/wiki/File%3AIberian_Lynx_front.jpg

By http://www.lynxexsitu.es , via Wikimedia Commons

http://commons.wikimedia.org/wiki/File%3ASalvador_Dali_NYWTS.jpg

By Roger Higgins, World Telegram staff photographer [Public domain], via Wikimedia Commons

All Other Photographs :

http://www.bigstockphoto.com

http://www.shutterstock.com

Glossary

adaptation – The term "adaption" refers to evolutionary changes over time that enable a species to better survive its circumstances and environment.

arboreal – Creatures that are arboreal spend the majority of their lives in trees.

critical habitat - A critical habitat is a defined geographic area that contains the features, both physical and biological, necessary for the species within the area to survive.

carnivore – Carnivores are animals in the order Carnivora, which is predominately made up of meat-eating mammals.

carrion – Carrion is comprised of the bodies of dead animals decaying in a natural state that are consumed by other animals.

contiguous forests – Any forests that share an edge or boundary are said to be contiguous.

crepuscular – Crepuscular animals are those that are most active at dawn or dusk. Many felid species are crepuscular although most of the small Central and South American cats are adaptable in this regard, responding to pressure from predators or the behavior of their primary prey.

deforestation - Deforestation is the process of destroying or clearing a forest in a permanent, long-term fashion.

depredation – Depredation is the act of wildlife preying upon a farmer's crops and/or livestock. Many of the small Central and South American cats, for instance, prey on poultry.

diurnal – Animals that are most active by day are said to be diurnal.

ecosystem – An ecosystem is made up of a group of organisms and their physical environment that interact as a unit.

endangered – When a species is in danger of extinction from any harmful factors in their environment they are said to be "endangered." Lesser designated categories for conservation purposes might be "threatened" or "special concern." Animals that face no threat are said to be of "least concern."

extinct - When no examples of a species exist anywhere on Earth the species is said to be extinct.

feral – Feral animals are domesticated animals that have returned to a wild state.

food chain – A food chain is a sequence of feeding types within a community ordered by successive levels. For instance, plants are eaten by rodents that are in turn eaten by wild cats and so forth.

forage – Forage is vegetation that is naturally consumed by herbivorous animals or is the act of searching for and eating such material.

gene pool – The gene pool is the total genetic information contained in a population of animals.

guard hairs – Guard hairs are long, coarse hairs that forms a protective coating over an animal's under fur and may stick up and give the creature a bushier appearance.

habitat - A habitat is the environment in which an animal lives naturally and normally lives and raises its offspring.

herbivore – An herbivore is an animal that eats a plant-based diet.

indigenous – A species of animal or plant that is a naturally occurring species for the region is said to be indigenous.

litter – A litter is the complete number of young born each time a female gives birth.

melanistic – Melanistic refers to an abnormally dark pigmentation of the skin or other tissues of an animal.

niche – A niche is the part of any habitat that is particularly suited to the survival requirements of a given species.

nocturnal – Animals that are primarily active at night are said to be nocturnal.

omnivore – Any animal that feeds on both plant and animal matter is said to be an omnivore.

pelage – The soft covering of any animal, including the hair, fur, and wool is called the pelage.

population – The total number of a species in a defined area is called the population.

range – Range is the geographic area or areas a species normally inhabits.

rare – Any species that is uncommon, limited to a restricted geographic area or habit, and is potentially at risk of extinction is said to be rare.

scat – Scat is the solid excrement dropped by an animal. Naturalist often study these droppings to learn more about an animals feeding patterns.

species – A species is comprised of populations of animals possessing common characteristics that freely inter-breed and produce fertile offspring that display the same characteristics.

territory – Territory refers to an animals dominance over a specific area of a habitat, which the creature usually defends against other members of its species and perhaps against other species as well. Animals breed, feed, and mate within their territories.

threatened – "Threatened" is a designation given to species when it is on the verge of becoming endangered in the foreseeable future.

Index

A

African Golden Cat 100, 101, 109, 110
African Wild Cat 101, 102, 103
Andean Cat 27, 28, 29, 30, 43, 132
arboreal 15, 16, 24, 97, 139, 141, 157
Argentina 5, 16, 20, 29, 31, 32, 36, 38, 39, 41, 45, 51, 111, 118, 137
armadillos 6, 139
Asian Golden Cat 67, 68, 69, 70, 90
Aztecs 2, 15

B

Bengals 125
binocular vision 132
Black-Footed Cat 38, 99, 103, 104
Bobcat 34, 50, 58, 60, 61, 62, 124
Bolivia 5, 20, 29, 31, 32, 43
Bornean Bay Cat 70, 90
Brazil 17, 20, 22, 32, 42, 43, 44, 45, 48, 49, 111, 138, 139, 140
burricon 20

C

Canadian Lynx 50, 62, 63, 64, 65, 66
capybara 139, 143
Caracal 72, 73, 74, 100, 109, 110
carnivores 24, 43, 61, 131, 157
catamount 51
caucel 20
Central America 5, 36, 45, 56
Chausie 90, 125
Chile 29, 38, 39, 40, 41, 42, 43, 53, 111
Chinchillidae 29
Chinese Desert Cat 75, 76
chivi 45
chulul 20
claws 84, 86, 88, 94, 132
Clouded Leopard 21, 77, 79
Colombia 5, 16, 20, 42, 45
color... 12, 29, 31, 88, 132, 140

color blind 132
Costa Rica 51
Cougar 51, 53, 56
crepuscular 29, 53, 60, 86, 92, 103, 107, 139, 157
cunaguaro 20

D

deer 6, 53, 61, 64, 69, 82, 101, 121, 139
dichromatic 132

E

Eastern Mexico 5
Ecuador 5, 20, 43, 45, 48, 111
El Salvador 13, 20
Eurasian Lynx 80, 82
Europe 49, 80, 98, 114, 115
eyes4, 11, 12, 16, 18, 23, 31, 35, 39, 42, 46, 47, 54, 56, 60, 62, 64, 66, 73, 75, 82, 84, 85, 86, 90, 92, 94, 100, 101, 113, 132, 133, 139, 142
Eyra 34

F

Felidae family 131
Fishing cat 134
Fishing Cat 83, 84, 86
Flat-Headed Cat 85, 86
forests 17, 32, 39, 52, 68, 76, 80, 88, 96, 137, 140, 157
fur 3, 13, 16, 19, 24, 28, 34, 37, 39, 40, 42, 46, 48, 62, 70, 76, 77, 78, 83, 86, 87, 93, 94, 95, 98, 100, 105, 113, 142, 159

G

gato de montes 20, 32
gato do mato 45
gato maracaja 20
gato montes 20
gato pintado 20
gato tigre 20, 45
Geoffroy's cat 133
Geoffroy's Cat 12, 27, 30, 31, 32, 33, 34, 48, 49, 134
gestation period ... 11, 47, 56, 62, 64, 66, 70, 74, 80, 82, 84, 86, 90, 92, 95, 98, 101, 103, 105, 113, 142
Guatemala 20
Guyana 5, 13, 45, 48

H

huamburushu 20
hybridization 48, 67, 114, 124, 126, 127

I

Iberian Lynx 114, 115, 116
IUCN Red List 44, 57, 96, 135

J

Jaguar 4, 8, 12, 52, 56, 58, 118, 121, 136, 137, 138, 139, 140, 141, 142, 143
Jaguarundi 12, 27, 34, 35, 37, 71, 118, 144
Jungle Cat 87, 89, 90, 125

K

kuichua 20

L

little spotted cat 45
little tiger cat 45

M

Marbled Cat 90, 92
Margay 1, 2, 12, 15, 16, 17, 19, 20, 21, 22, 24, 25, 26, 27, 44, 47, 124, 129, 130, 133, 135
mbaracaya 20
mirim peludo 20
mythology 2, 51, 136

N

nocturnal .. 7, 18, 29, 33, 39, 43, 47, 63, 71, 86, 89, 92, 97, 103, 104, 107, 112, 126, 139, 159
Northern Andes 5

O

Ocelot 1, 2, 3, 4, 5, 6, 7, 8, 9, 10, 11, 12, 13, 15, 17, 19, 24, 26, 27, 44, 118, 119, 121, 123, 124, 129, 130, 135, 136
Oncilla 27, 32, 44, 45, 46, 47, 48, 124, 135

P

Pallas's Cat 93, 94, 95

Paraguay 5, 20, 31, 32, 42, 43, 111

Patagonian Andes 32

peccaries 139, 143

Peru 9, 13, 20, 29, 43, 45, 48, 111

pets 123, 124, 125, 126, 127

pichigueta 20

predators 12, 24, 58, 61, 63, 64, 65, 70, 74, 79, 90, 97, 134, 138, 141, 143, 157

prey 5, 6, 8, 9, 12, 24, 29, 33, 46, 48, 52, 53, 56, 61, 64, 65, 69, 70, 74, 76, 79, 82, 84, 86, 90, 92, 93, 94, 103, 104, 105, 106, 107, 109, 113, 114, 115, 116, 121, 131, 132, 133, 134, 138, 142, 143, 157, 158

Puma 8, 12, 34, 50, 51, 52, 53, 54, 55, 56, 57, 142

R

rainforests 2, 9, 45, 137, 141

Rusty Spotted Cat 96, 98

S

Safari 34, 125

Salvador Dali 123

Savannah 99, 125

Serengeti 125

skin 46, 92, 131, 132, 159

South America 1, 16, 30, 31, 34, 43, 45, 49, 50, 51, 55, 71, 131

Southern Arizona 5, 137

Southern Texas 5

spotted cats 2, 12, 14, 26, 124, 125, 136

T

tail 3, 4, 10, 19, 22, 28, 29, 31, 32, 35, 38, 39, 42, 46, 51, 54, 55, 58, 60, 68, 70, 73, 76, 78, 80, 83, 84, 90, 91, 93, 96, 100, 102, 103, 105, 109, 110, 132, 133, 140

tamarin 22

tapirs 139

Tezcatlipoca 2, 136

The IUCN (The International Union for Conservation of Nature) 37

tigre gallinero 45

tigrillito 20

tigrillo 20, 45

tigrillo peludo 45

tirica 45

Trinidad 5, 121

U

Uruguay 16, 20, 25, 31, 36, 42, 43, 111

V

Venezuela 5, 20, 45, 139, 140
vibrissae.. 133

W

whiskers.. 133

Notes:

CPSIA information can be obtained
at www.ICGtesting.com
Printed in the USA
BVHW050214310120
570973BV00002B/23